Decolonisation and the Law School

This book explores strategies, approaches, tools, challenges, and reflections that animate the conversation around decolonisation in UK law schools. It investigates how we can have, within the UK law school, difficult conversations about the ways in which history has influenced what the law is, how law is taught, what law is taught, who the law works for, and who the law does not work for.

The conversation about decolonisation of the university and curricula continues to raise questions for knowledge production and transmission in educational institutions. Decolonisation also raises questions about the impact of the preceding issues on people within and outside these educational institutions. The decolonisation debate is an opportunity for legal academics to reflect on the origins of their own individual academic practices in research as well as the content of their curriculum. This volume examines the preceding issues as they relate to academic practices and legal pedagogy in UK law schools. The authors examine how legal scholars can achieve aims of decolonisation within the practical objectives of teaching of law as well as the limitations and possible challenges of these endeavours.

This volume will be of interest to legal scholars, legal educators, law students, and legal practitioners who are engaged in questions of how decolonisation relates to law – both broadly understood. It was originally published as a special issue of *The Law Teacher.*

Foluke I. Adebisi is Professor of Law at the University of Bristol Law School, UK. Her scholarship on decolonisation and legal pedagogy responds to the question of what it means to be human.

Decolonisation and the Law School

Dreaming Beyond Aesthetic Changes to the Curriculum

Edited by
Foluke I. Adebisi

Routledge
Taylor & Francis Group
LONDON AND NEW YORK

First published 2024
by Routledge
4 Park Square, Milton Park, Abingdon, Oxon, OX14 4RN

and by Routledge
605 Third Avenue, New York, NY 10158

Routledge is an imprint of the Taylor & Francis Group, an informa business

British Library Cataloguing in Publication Data
A catalogue record for this book is available from the British Library

ISBN13: 978-1-032-77118-2 (hbk)
ISBN13: 978-1-032-77120-5 (pbk)
ISBN13: 978-1-003-48132-4 (ebk)

DOI: 10.4324/9781003481324

Typeset in Myriad Pro
by codeMantra

Publisher's Note
The publisher accepts responsibility for any inconsistencies that may have arisen during the conversion of this book from journal articles to book chapters, namely the inclusion of journal terminology.

Disclaimer
Every effort has been made to contact copyright holders for their permission to reprint material in this book. The publishers would be grateful to hear from any copyright holder who is not here acknowledged and will undertake to rectify any errors or omissions in future editions of this book.

Contents

Citation Information vii
Notes on Contributors ix

Introduction: Decolonisation and the law school: presences, absences, silences… and hope 1
Foluke I. Adebisi

1 Trust, courage and silence: carving out decolonial spaces in higher education through student–staff partnerships 7
Ahmed Raza Memon and Suhraiya Jivraj

2 "Law", "order", "justice", "crime": disrupting key concepts in criminology through the study of colonial history 21
J.M. Moore

3 Creating the law school as a meeting place for epistemologies: decolonising the teaching of jurisprudence and human rights 35
Sophie Rigney

4 Researching colonialism and colonial legacies from a legal perspective 49
Nandini S. Boodia-Canoo

5 "Why is it my problem if they don't take part?" The (non)role of white academics in decolonising the law school 64
Nick Cartwright and T.O. Cartwright

6 Decolonising the master's house: how Black Feminist epistemologies can be and are used in decolonial strategy 79
Oluwaseun Matiluko

7 The ignored heritage of Western law: the historical and contemporary role of Islamic law in shaping law schools 94
Imranali Panjwani

Index 111

Citation Information

The chapters in this book were originally published in the journal *The Law Teacher*, volume 54, issue 4 (2020). When citing this material, please use the original page numbering for each article, as follows:

Chapter 1

Trust, courage and silence: carving out decolonial spaces in higher education through student–staff partnerships
Ahmed Raza Memon and Suhraiya Jivraj
The Law Teacher, volume 54, issue 4 (2020), pp. 475–488

Chapter 2

"Law", "order", "justice", "crime": disrupting key concepts in criminology through the study of colonial history
J.M. Moore
The Law Teacher, volume 54, issue 4 (2020), pp. 489–502

Chapter 3

Creating the law school as a meeting place for epistemologies: decolonising the teaching of jurisprudence and human rights
Sophie Rigney
The Law Teacher, volume 54, issue 4 (2020), pp. 503–516

Chapter 4

Researching colonialism and colonial legacies from a legal perspective
Nandini S. Boodia-Canoo
The Law Teacher, volume 54, issue 4 (2020), pp. 517–531

Chapter 5

"Why is it my problem if they don't take part?" The (non)role of white academics in decolonising the law school
Nick Cartwright and T.O. Cartwright
The Law Teacher, volume 54, issue 4 (2020), pp. 532–546

Chapter 6

Decolonising the master's house: how Black Feminist epistemologies can be and are used in decolonial strategy
Oluwaseun Matiluko
The Law Teacher, volume 54, issue 4 (2020), pp. 547–561

Chapter 7

The ignored heritage of Western law: the historical and contemporary role of Islamic law in shaping law schools
Imranali Panjwani
The Law Teacher, volume 54, issue 4 (2020), pp. 562–577

Notes on Contributors

Foluke I. Adebisi, University of Bristol Law School, UK.

Nandini S. Boodia-Canoo, Lawyer and an academic.

Nick Cartwright, Law, University of Northampton, UK.

T.O. Cartwright, Independent Scholar.

Suhraiya Jivraj, University of Kent, Canterbury, UK.

Oluwaseun Matiluko, Graduate, Law School, University of Bristol, UK.

J.M. Moore, Hertfordshire Law School, University of Hertfordshire, UK.

Imranali Panjwani, Law Lecturer, Faculty of Business and Law, Anglia Ruskin University, Chelmsford, UK.

Ahmed Raza Memon, the School of Law and Politics at Cardiff University, UK.

Sophie Rigney, Indigenous Law Centre, Faculty of Law, University of New South Wales, Sydney, Australia.

Introduction: Decolonising the law school: presences, absences, silences... and hope

Foluke I. Adebisi

Introduction

Decolonisation has meant many things to many people at different times and places. Currently a lot of the discourse around decolonisation in UK Higher Education (HE) has involved including more topics or readings from people from racialised or colonised backgrounds – in other words performative and sometimes harmful moves to diversify. Consequently, many scholars who work in this area have suggested, very strongly, that decolonisation invites much more materiality than being a synonym for cosmetic diversity. As such, the invitation to "decolonise the law school" can be perceived as an invitation to acknowledge that the legal history which created our present realities has not always been benign or kind. So, we should not engage with decolonisation without acknowledging the work of past and present imperial projects – and more specifically, especially in the context of the UK law school, the work of the British Empire. The invitation to decolonise does not only have an interest in the afterlives of empire, but it also invites us to heavily invest in the world we can build in that afterlife, that breaks from what has come before. In other words, the colonial project – its inception dated to the 15th century and its trajectory still ongoing around us – has provoked decolonisation as a response. Decolonisation in this guise requires a direct and engaged refusal of colonialism's unequal and destructive ways of living that produce racial injustice, extreme inequality, and planetary collapse. This volume seeks to explore how we can have, within the UK law school, difficult conversations about the ways in which history has influenced what the law is, how law is taught, what law is taught, who the law works for, and who the law does not work for.

What on earth is decolonisation?

Decolonisation, as an epistemological term, has various schools of thought that are often socio-politically context-dependent and sometimes discipline-specific. For example, Tuck and Yang's incisive essay, written from the context of indigenous peoples in Canada, tells us very categorically that decolonisation means nothing less than the return of stolen land.[1] Scholars often designated as post/anticolonial writers, e.g. Homi Bhabha and Nkrumah, mostly engage in temporally situated analyses of the material

[1]Tuck, Eve, and K. Wayne Yang. 'Decolonization Is Not a Metaphor'. *Decolonization: Indigeneity, Education & Society* 1, no. 1 (8 September 2012): 1–40.

and immaterial aspects and effects of imperial territorial control and how this control required and requires for survival, particular knowledge articulations and ontological presumptions.[2] In other words, postcolonial theory influences an articulation of decolonisation that addresses specific enduring injustices that exist within the postcolonial context from which each articulation of decolonisation emerges. From the Latin American critical school, comes the idea of "coloniality" – as a state of global being that underpins our ways of thinking and doing in the world. The architects of coloniality manufactured and weaponised the evolving social category of "race" as a technology of extraction, destruction, and rupture.[3] All these articulations of decolonisation recognise that there are other ways of thinking and living that are not predicted on the destruction of human bodies and bodies of knowledge as well as the centring and superiorisation of European bodies of thought. As such, across these schools of thought, decolonisation can be understood as being undergirded by material and epistemic repudiations of the colonial that seek within their positions an "after-colonial" time and reality. In essence, decolonisation is an immediate, multivariate, continuing, and stubborn refusal of colonial conditions of domination, dispossession, and dehumanisation, as well as of the epistemologies that keep coloniality eternally reemergent. Thus, we must understand that decolonisation is not curricula/research redesign or innovation but an invitation to redesign our work so that it redesigns our world. So, rather than pose the question, "How can I decolonise my curriculum?", we can ask instead, "What does it mean to dream of new anticolonial worlds from within the law school?"[4] Survival is being threatened on a planetary scale through among other things the combined forces of global inequality, racial violence, and climate change. But as long as we are still here, as long as we can still breathe, we must dream of more beautiful worlds.

Whiter the law school and its colonial discipline? Law as global design

Decolonisation forces us to confront the history and effects of imperialism upon our academic practices in law as well as the nature of law itself. To understand how the conditions of life introduced and globalised by colonialism have become normalised and woven into the structures that reproduce the current world, it is important to understand the role of Euro-modern law in shaping global structures as well as human behaviour and standards. Without a detailed examination of this, decolonisation will fail to properly engage with the realities that the law produces and fail to produce a "world otherwise." As legal academics, it is imperative that we explore what decolonisation means for us and what the possibility of decolonisation and law means for the relationship between law and society as well as the life of a law school. Decolonisation is also a reflective practice in which we as academics must constantly adapt our own pedagogies and question our own practices. For example, we can reflect on the following questions: How do we become more aware of, and directly mention, how the law came to be, in tandem with a history of legalised dispossession of land and

---

[2]Nkrumah, Kwame. *Neo-colonialism: The Last Stage of Imperialism*. International Publishers, 1966.

[3]Quijano, Aníbal. 'Coloniality of Power and Eurocentrism in Latin America'. *International Sociology* 15, no. 2 (1 June 2000): 215–32.

[4]Adébísí, Folúkẹ́. *Decolonisation and Legal Knowledge: Reflections on Power and Possibility*. Bristol University Press, 2023,129.

personhood as well as an othering from humanity? How do we teach law as the study of social order and elucidate how racial and gendered stratifications in the social are formed and maintained? How do we show to our students, in very concrete terms, exactly how the past bleeds into the present, how we walk side by side with histories' ghosts, how we breathe coloniality every day, and how our collective history is literally present in every single thing we do? It is this history that describes law as a colonial discipline within which bodies and space-time have been revalued and redefined to meet the needs of enclosure, property-making, and capital accumulation. Thus, we must deconstruct the complicity of law in enabling colonially and racially accumulated capital and other advantages to be retained.[5] The aims of this volume and the conference from which it emerged were to open a conversation among legal scholars that could begin to respond to the foregoing questions and to pose new ones.

The conference and the keynote

On the 13th of September 2019, I convened at the Law School, University of Bristol, a conference titled, "Decolonisation and the Law School." The purpose of the conference was to bring together some of the vast array of decolonial work legal academics across the UK were doing. We were particularly interested in how they were bringing this work into their teaching and their research.

The keynote address, titled "Cacophony, Autocritique and Abolition: Impression points on decolonisation and the Law School,"[6] was delivered by Joel Modiri, (then) a Senior Lecturer in the Department of Jurisprudence, University of Pretoria, South Africa. It was vital for us to include excerpts [with permission] from the keynote address in this collection as the keynote provided an insightful perspective and framing from a jurisdiction which has gone further with their approaches to decolonisation in legal education than we have here in the UK.

In his address, Modiri pointed out how decolonisation had become watered down/ confused:

> "decolonisation" has risen to prominence as the supervening motif and buzzword employed by academics and universities struggling to respond to the accumulated contradictions of colonial, imperial and racial histories – thrown into sharper relief by the world-historical students protests of 2015–2017, but always lingering in varied political struggles and intellectual traditions... The almost ritualistic invocation of the notion of decolonisation situates it nervously between a critical zeitgeist that discloses productive, radical and disruptive directions for knowledge production and a gratuitous referent for platitudinous, opportunistic and vacuous scholarship. The reduction of decolonisation into a 'mainstream' metaphor for social justice and curriculum transformation delinks it from pressing material realities and struggles faced by indigenous and racially oppressed communities – a critique made famous by Eve Tuck and K Wayne Yang. Crucially, as a term of political justice, 'decolonisation' must also retain its oppositional and subversive character – especially in relation to whiteness.

---

[5] Adebisi, Foluke. 'Black/African Science Fiction and the Quest for Racial Justice through Legal Knowledge: How Can We Unsettle Euro-Modern Time and Temporality in Our Teaching?' *Law, Technology and Humans* 4, no. 2 (14 November 2022): 24–37.

[6] The text of this keynote has been published in more detail in 'The Aporias of Decolonisation in the South African academy' in Olawaseun Tella and S Motala (eds.) *Transforming Ivory Towers to Ebony Towers: Transforming Humanities Curricula in South Africa, Africa and African-American Studies.* South Africa, 2020, 157–173.

The above confusion he says is compounded by the seizure of decolonisation by the capitalist ends of neoliberal universities, Modiri noted:

> the capture of decolonisation within the institutional and bureaucratic structures of the neoliberal university – and especially the relentless commodification, branding, marketisation, and professionalization of critical knowledges. Here, the challenge is for decolonisation to remain in tension with the neoliberal university – outside of and against its metrics and mechanisms. Decolonisation and decommodification of higher education are thus intricately linked.

This tension raises the question of the [im]possibility of decolonisation, he pointed out:

> the impossibility of a completely decolonized university in a still Eurocentric and capitalist modern world order shaped by centuries-long unfoldment of global white supremacy. This is further complicated by David Scott's reminder that colonial modernity has not only left its mark on the material and symbolic world as an order of oppression, violence and dehumanisation but has also produced, that is, conscripted, the very subjects called to resist and overthrow it.

Thus, decolonising knowledge is more fundamental and intricate than ticking a box:

> Navigating these dilemmas and aporias in all this cacophony requires not only that we withstand the seeming risks, complexities and impossibilities of decolonisation but also to be self-critical (autocritical) about our positions, practices and perspectives as we do the work of decolonising curricula, pedagogies, symbols and institutional cultures of our universities. This of course has to be part of a larger struggle to decolonize and dismantle material power relations in our societies and the world at large.

In discussing what decolonising of knowledge means, Modiri drew on the work of Linda Tuhiwai Smith:

> An alternative, more apposite, standpoint or orientation can be found in the work of Linda Tuhiwai Smith who has developed a methodology for the decolonisation of knowledge production, storytelling and theory building that is centred on the recovery of an indigenous perspective and an overturning of the Western gaze. Tuhiwai Smith delineates a series of "indigenous projects" which she advances as tools for contesting the social reality that sustains (legal) knowledge.

He pointed out that talking about decolonisation within the law raised questions of law's ontology and historical use:

> Robert A. Williams has argued that the Western colonising nations of Europe and their derivative settler-colonial states (such as South Africa, the United States, Australia, and Canada) have been sustained by the civilisational conceit that Western cultures, religions and civilisation are far superior to the religions, cultures and knowledges of non-Western peoples. It is an almost trite point of anticolonial, decolonial and postcolonial critique that it was this idea of European civilizational superiority that consecrated the "West's mandate to conquer the earth". But what Williams adds to this account is the role of law in this regard. Williams explains that in the Western imagination, the law is valued as "a respected and cherished instrument of civilisation" and served historically as "the West's most vital and effective instrument of empire", as a way of authoritatively "imposing [Europe's] particular vision of truth" on indigenous conquered peoples across the world. **Euro-Western law and jurisprudence is inseparable from colonial racism, dispossession and violence.**

His address then drew upon the South African experience and effect of colonial law within that:

> Often forgotten yet painfully obvious in legal education and legal study is the fact that South African law today is composed largely of Western traditions of liberal constitutionalism combined with the law of the colonial settler imposed through Dutch and British conquest of South Africa. The vaunted plurality of laws in the present constitutional dispensation conceals the marginalization and denigration of indigenous African law – which is marked as particular and frequently cast in a civilizational narrative as being in tension with progress, development and rights, being relegated and distorted from history into the present. Martin Chanock further points out that South African common law was central to the "creation of white memory and [the] racial and national identity" of European settlers. When this is compounded with the demographic whiteness of the legal academy and the Eurocentrism of South African jurisprudence scholars, it can thus be easily said that South African law is in fact "white law".
>
> South African law's historical unfoldment as part a larger project of a "dark modernity" comprising European supremacy, racial capitalism and sexism and its development – substantively and procedurally – in the cauldron of slavery, colonisation and apartheid, has considerable bearing on how its operative concepts are understood and actualised, such as for example how and by whom disputes are adjudicated; what constitutes a family; the meaning and character of personhood; how relations of property (affecting contract and succession) are established and enforced; how obligations are formed and discharged; what modes of statecraft and governance are employed; how tensions between law and cultural traditions ought to be reconciled; how transgressions of the law and community values are addressed and penalised; how the division between the public and private is formulated and so on. **To draw on law, rights and courts as tools for the achievement of equality and justice risks ignoring the historical and cultural problematicity of this law – the fact that it embeds a cultural framework rooted in racism - and to thereby deepen the colonial unknowing**. Legal reform in this case requires the objectionable suspension of the demand for epistemic justice, for African law to assume its proper place as "law equal to any law anywhere on our planet Earth".

Modiri ended his address with a reminder of the long intellectual history and fundamental purposes of decolonial thought in universities:

> the contemporary university is organised by neoliberal logics that threaten to commodify and hence depoliticise those emancipatory knowledges and institutionalize them within its largely conservative disciplinary structures. The meaning and possibilities of decolonisation would be severely eroded if it is reduced to a metaphor for the merely conceptual and rhetorical exercise of revising curricula, diversifying the professoriate and redesigning spaces. In the result, **decolonisation would wither into a demand to belong to the universities but not yet for the universities to belong to us** and we would be interpellated into adopting minoritarian vocabularies and sensibilities at odds with the liberatory impulse of decolonisation.
>
> To maintain fidelity to the great ideals of the anti-colonial wars of resistance and the revolutionary political and intellectual traditions of anti-colonialism and antiracism which have followed in their wake, we must hold on to the aporetic promises of decolonisation – its most combative and most capacious imaginings. **Decolonisation is an insatiable reparatory demand, an insurrectionary utterance, that always exceeds the temporality and scene of its enunciation. It entails nothing less than an endless fracturing of the world colonialism created.**

A summary of this volume

Some of the papers delivered at the conference are contained here. The overarching aim of creating this scholastic record is to illustrate how approaches to decolonisation require engagement with practice and theorisation of concepts of decolonisation that are grounded in the pre-existing literature and linked to the history of Empire. In a lot of the discourse on decolonisation in UK Higher Education, tools such as diversity and inclusion have been adopted with a narrow focus only on practice and teaching to the detriment of theory and research. Yet, efficient utilisation of decolonisation's ideas in teaching requires a good grounding in theoretical articulation of the concept.[7]

This collection includes contributions on praxis, theory, unit development, extra-curricular decolonising, and personal reflection. John Moore uses his experience of teaching a unit with the diverse literature to illustrate the colonial underpinnings of criminology. Sophie Rigney's article explores the jurisprudence of person and place in teaching about indigenous knowledge. Suhraiya Jivraj and Ahmed Raza Memon reflect on how a collaborative project with students demonstrates decolonial knowledge production. Oluwaseun Matiliuko recommends the use of Black Feminist Theory to decolonise teaching in law schools. Imranali Panjwali investigates the jurisprudence of Islamic law with specific reference to the teaching of EU law. Nandini Boodia-Canoo uses Mauritius as an example of why legal historical research should include colonial law. Teleola Cartwright and Nick Cartwright reflect on how positionality of academics affects their recommended progress through decolonial praxis.

I hope you enjoy reading this special issue. I hope it will enable us to build on and implement our dreams of a better and fairer world. For our dreams for the world are currently too small, our visions currently too limited, our structures unwise, unsustainable, and unsafe. We must let our dreams and visions do more than continually reproduce an uneven world – a world where the lots of those who must die so that others may live and have always been unfairly cast.

I conclude by extending my thanks to all the contributors and reviewers; the Society of Legal Scholars and the Law School at the University of Bristol who funded the conference financially and logistically; The Editorial Board of the Law Teacher; and Chris Willmore and Tonia Novitz for planting the idea of the conference and the special issue, for their support, and for their encouragement.

[7]For more examples of this, see Adebisi, Foluke, Suhraiya Jivraj, and Ntina Tzouvala, eds. *Decolonisation, Anti-Racism, and Legal Pedagogy: Strategies, Successes, and Challenges*. 1st edition. Routledge, 2023.

Trust, courage and silence: carving out decolonial spaces in higher education through student–staff partnerships

Ahmed Raza Memon and Suhraiya Jivraj

ABSTRACT

On 20 March 2019, the Decolonise UoK, formerly Decolonise UKC conference took place at the University of Kent (W Ahmed and others, Decolonising the Curriculum Project Manifesto: Through the Kaleidoscope (2019) <https://decoloniseukc.files.wordpress.com/2019/03/decolonising-the-curriculum-manifesto-final-2.pdf). Out of this came its manifesto to the university with recommendations in three key areas (ibid). The end goal of this student–staff collaboration was not intended to be a strategic intervention to equality, diversity and inclusion (EDI) work within universities although the body of knowledge (the manifesto and the Decolonise UoK Collective book, *Towards Decolonising the University: A Kaleidoscope for Empowered Action* (Counterpress 2020)) is open access for everyone to read and implement. We explore this process of self-empowerment through the concepts of (re-)existence/resistance from decolonial studies in combination with the black feminist critical race theory (CRT) methods of counter-narrating. We discuss the detail of racialised life both as part of surviving and through resisting institutional racism and its affective impact upon us. We argue that the necessary conditions that made it possible to do the work of self-empowerment from our intersectional and multiple positionalities across the student–staff continuum within the neoliberal university have been trust, courage and silence.

1. Introduction

In the wake of the 2015 UK based decolonise student movements at UCL and SOAS[1] like many other universities the University of Kent Student Union began a campaign to "diversify the curriculum" which was not taken forward. In 2018 I (Suhraiya) devised a "teaching enhancement innovation" pilot gaining university funding to launch it from my third-year optional module "Race, Religion and Law". Devising the project – which the students later named Decolonise UKC and then UoK – was very much an act of resisting the "BME attainment gaps" narratives which in my view only served to perpetuate racialisation rather than address it.[2] The gap narrative did not reflect the truth of what I had experienced with students in my classes or that I encountered more

[1]"Decolonising the Curriculum: What's All the Fuss About?" <www.soas.ac.uk/blogs/study/decolonising-curriculum-whats-the-fuss/ accessed 29 June 2020.

[2]Decolonise UoK Collective, *Towards Decolonising the University: A Kaleidoscope for Empowered Action* (Counterpress 2020).

broadly in different universities over the last decade. I knew already that the voices of my own students coming through their work certainly defied the dominant "deficit" presumptions despite all the structural hurdles they face. I wanted to work with those students to *co-produce* knowledge which could inform pedagogy and policy across the law school and beyond. However, the underlying impetus was to empower them to become researchers, knowledge producers and stakeholders in their own education. To that end we trained and guided "Focus Group Leaders" who were all members of the Decolonise UoK Collective through the research and ethics process to conduct café-style group discussions. In addition to these group discussions which included 80 students, they conducted one-to-one interviews with students who did not feel "comfortable" in a group session, including for fear of being surveilled. The Decolonise UoK manifesto documents the data from these focus groups and interviews. It reflected experiences and made recommendations that echo those highlighted by other student campaigns to decolonise or liberate the curriculum, such as lack of diversity in reading lists and the need for tackling overt racism and micro-aggressions experienced in and outside the classroom. However, the Decolonise UoK manifesto also spoke to their individualised experiences within the locality of Kent which is the border frontier of Brexit Britain and with little ethnic diversity in population – apart from students – despite being so close to London where many of the students have come from. These specifics have been particularly salient to issues such as the lack of culturally sensitive provision of wellbeing services, lack of accessible channels for tackling racism in the face of a rise in fascist, Islamophobic, anti-Semitic and anti-immigration activity and rhetoric on campus, whilst also facing increasing surveillance on campus by security staff as a result of the Prevent Duty and continued societal racism particularly towards black men and Muslims.[3] In this context it is no surprise that students experience a sense of dysphoria rather than belonging, without ostensible institutional support and few staff of colour which we know to be crucial for students so they can see themselves reflected in the teaching staff around them. Within this context the importance of student–staff connections in creating conditions for learning cannot be overstated. Collaborating on co-producing knowledge is one way to facilitate this but requires different affective resources than those that have taken place in the colonial metropolis of London.

As academic lead (Suhraiya) for the project and a PhD student and staff member teaching at the university (Ahmed) we have reflected on the project over the course of two years through our own collaboration conducting workshops and trainings at other universities and law schools. These included the "Building the Anti-Racist Classroom Collective" (BARC) workshop at Leeds Beckett University where we participated and led a long-table session,[4] presenting at a Decolonising Law workshop at the University of Bristol, an interactive workshop with law school staff at the University of Warwick and another workshop at the University of Reading in 2020. Keeping this in mind then, decolonising the university for us is at its heart about building a decolonial space for resistance as re-existence. We discuss not just *how* we think the space has been a "decolonial space" but what we believe is required in the making a *space* like this in the

[3] Wahida and others, *Decolonising the Curriculum Project Manifesto: Through the Kaleidoscope* (2019) <https://decoloniseukc.files.wordpress.com/2019/03/decolonising-the-curriculum-manifesto-final-2.pdf>.

[4] Building the Anti-Racist Classroom Collective, Organising for Liberation Workshop (Leeds Beckett University, 2019).

first place: namely, the conditions that such a space would be contingent upon. Our continued collaborations in all these formats allowed us to reflect upon and reimagine the way in which the project had a life of its own that emerged from rare space within the university that was built upon conditions of trust, courage and silence. We argue that a decolonial space needs to first understand both the importance of but also the need for a student/staff relationality. This is particularly important within a decolonial space as it informs how we understand the university and the "mistrust" already present in the relationship between students and the university.

After a brief explanation of our methodology, we elaborate on these elements of "trust", "courage" and "silence". In our section on the elements of *trust*, while referring to lived experiences of building the space, we also show how the environment to do so needs to be created where the student–staff dynamic is one of "relationality" of care and nurturing.[5] In the sections on *courage* and *silence*, we show how the re-existence/rebuilding acts in itself as a dismantling of racist capitalist structures of the colonial university. In the section on courage we explore how the "challenges" to build a space itself are part of having "courage" and how this is entangled with finding different modes of expression beyond academic forms and particularly through legacies of radical revolutionaries. This informs our understanding, in the next section, of how we conceptualise *silence* in the face of whiteness. We argue that while breaking the silence of a neoliberal colonial university is dependent on having "trust" and "courage", we also need to be aware of *how* silencing operates in different guises, even through well-meaning white alliances. Furthermore, we also ask if any form of institutional or academic expression – regardless of its critical, radical or anti-colonial aim – ends up reproducing a *silencing* and coloniality in another form.

We conclude with final reflections on what the place of "decolonial space" is within a neoliberal colonial university – and what it means for us (staff and students) to be a part of its structure. Reflecting on our methodological and theoretical coalescing of critical race theory's main tenets of lived experience along with decolonial thought's understanding of decolonisation of self and re-existence, our concluding reflection on ethics builds on this reading of both literatures together. The reflections we put forward may provide other student and staff collaboration groups thinking of creating a decolonial space with some important reflections to take away, particularly given the context of marketisation of "decolonising/anti racism" in the colonial neoliberal university.

Decoloniality and critical race theory: methodology

This reflection is informed through theoretical reading of how racism is understood and explained through critical race theory (CRT) as well as decolonial studies. We draw on personal experiences, anecdotes, recalling of moments which is both theoretically and methodologically informed by CRT's key tenet of understanding lived experience as knowledge, whilst analysing that knowledge through decolonial theorisations of coloniality and resistance.[6] Additionally, we argue that CRT's explanation of racism and racist structures can be informed by and furthered through the use of decolonial

[5]Suhraiya Jivraj, "Decolonizing the Academy – Between a Rock and a Hard Place" (2020) 22 Interventions 552.

[6]Gloria Ladson-Billings and William F Tate, "Toward a Critical Race Theory of Education" in Adrienne Dixson and others (eds), *Critical Race Theory in Education* (Routledge 2018); Gloria Ladson-Billings, "Just What Is Critical Race Theory and What's It Doing in a Nice Field Like Education?" (1998) 11 International Journal of Qualitative Studies in Education 7; Bell Hooks, *Teaching to Transgress* (Routledge 2014).

scholarship to explore building a decolonial space as a form of re-existence as resistance. The aim of transnational decolonial scholarship, particularly through reading of Walter Mignolo, Sylvia Wynter, Ali Shariati, amongst others is to understand "decolonising" as a process that can facilitate (re-)existence, which is part of and not separate from resistance within and against the neoliberal colonial university.[7] We discuss decoloniality here as a process of deconstructing the colonised self while reasserting a form of intellectual, emotional, spiritual re-existence.[8] It enables us to understand the significance of material and micro structures (lived/everyday) to macro(structural) oppressive forms of exploitation apparent from our own experiences of Decolonise UoK over the last two years. This understanding does not preclude dismantling racial/oppressive hierarchies embedded through/within capitalism, but contends that decolonisation, in the form of dismantling racial capitalism through the economic and territorial, needs to go hand in hand with decolonising of the colonised self while creating space for re-existence.

2. "Mistrust" and enduring coloniality of the university

As a student, I (Ahmed) recall very well how Suhraiya and Dave – another staff facilitator – gave very early indications of this shifting from what was familiar. The familiar was an institutional approach ingrained in the nature of a neoliberal university model where the hierarchy of student–staff is dictated by the specific purpose of "assessing" the value of students – or "clients" – in order to give them a return for their "investment". The institutionalised relation already comes with its preconditions, its expectations from its "customers/clients". These preconditions and expectations put physical, intellectual, and social distance between the teachers and the students. Through lack of transparency, a "formal" homogenous interaction with "students" as an abstract general "body" rather than individuals with social, personal, intellectual and emotional lives is instituted. University metrics that dictate these preconditions, whether they are Teaching Excellence Framework (TEF), Research Excellence Framework (REF) and Knowledge Excellence Framework (KEF) or equality, diversity and inclusion (EDI) policies, are all part of this interaction which for the most part students have no knowledge of, let alone the degree to which it affects their lives. In fact, as Akile Ahmet rightly points out, conversations on "inclusive pedagogy" are tacked on to diversification and EDI policies to reiterate the "dominant institutional culture embedded in whiteness, able bodies, and heteronormativity".[9]

---

[7] See for example, L Elena Delgado, Rolando J Romero and Walter Mignolo, "Local Histories and Global Designs: An Interview with Walter Mignolo" (2000) 22(3) Discourse 7; Walter D Mignolo, "Epistemic Disobedience, Independent Thought and Decolonial Freedom" (2009) 26(7–8) Theory, Culture & Society 159; Walter Mignolo, "Foreword: Decolonial Body-Geo-Politics at Large" in Sandeep Bakshi, Suhraiya Jivraj and Silvia Posocco (eds), *Decolonizing Sexualities: Transnational Perspectives, Critical Interventions* (Counterpress 2016) 7–18; Kaiama L Glover, "Sylvia Wynter: On Being Human as Praxis" (2016) 10 Contemporary Women's Writing 145; Ali Shariati, "Modern Man and His Prisons" in *Man and Islam* (North Haledon: Islamic Publications International 1981) 46–62. This includes and is not limited to Islamic philosopher, Allama Iqbal's conceptualisation of colonialism in Iqbal Singh Sevea, *The Political Philosophy of Muhammad Iqbal: Islam and Nationalism in Late Colonial India* (Cambridge University Press 2014).

[8] Cedric J Robinson, *Black Marxism: The Making of the Black Radical Tradition* (Univ of North Carolina Press 2000-). Robin DG Kelley, "What Did Cedric Robinson Mean by Racial Capitalism?" *The Boston Review* (2016) <bostonreview.net/race/robin-d-g-kelley-what-did-cedric-robinson-meanracial-capitalism> accessed 03 June 2020 .

[9] Akile Ahmet, "What Exactly Are Inclusive Pedagogies?" (29 June 2020) <https://blogs.lse.ac.uk/highereducation/2020/06/29/what-exactly-are-inclusive-pedagogies/>.

Through understanding how these policies both use metrics and other standards as part of a university's continuing efforts to maintain institutional racism we can also look at the university more squarely in terms of what some scholars have referred to as the "plantation politics" of higher education (HE).[10] Cheryl Matias has described her experience as a woman of colour in academy as "nothing more than a neoplantation" in which there is use/abuse of the body for the material benefit of the university where faces and bodies of faculty of colour are sold to college websites for statistical data.[11] Similarly students from Decolonise UoK and other student decolonise movements that took place at the Stories of (Un)belonging event[12] articulated frustration with being "paraded" and "co-opted" when it suited the universities' marketing strategies, particularly to recruit more "BAME" students. This part of the university's neoliberal machinations is often hidden from students, yet staff (of colour) will be aware of it and be part of constantly "keeping up an institutional face". Matias further describes this:

> we must sit next to white administrators who expect us to behave like uncle toms . . . under the surveilling eyes of the college administration, like trained dogs, we are expected to bark a false romance of being faculty of colour in the academy.[13]

In the context of the United Kingdom, students and staff can become subsumed under the "plantation" politics of the university,[14] often leaving many of us feeling anxiety, stress and exhaustion as a result of "racial battle fatigue".[15] Thus while neoliberalisation of the university is viewed through a paradigm of continuing commodification of education which suggests the creation of a consumer–producer relationship,[16] from the perspective of staff of colour, higher education policy needs also to be understood through structures of racial capitalism[17] or more squarely as "neoplantations".[18] The homogenous consumer or student and producer or university hides the structures through which the colonial neoliberal logics of the university operate to perpetuate institutional racism. Students are not just "consumers", the student as a consumer, investor and benefactor was always the white, upper-class cis male as opposed to those who did not belong in that category. HE has always been embedded within colonial, racist logics within itself in different forms.[19]

---

[10]T Elon Dancy, Kirsten T Edwards and James Earl Davis, "Historically White Universities and Plantation Politics: Anti-Blackness and Higher Education in the Black Lives Matter Era" (2018) 53 Urban Education 176; Dian Squire, Bianca C Williams and Frank Tuitt, "Plantation Politics and Neoliberal Racism in Higher Education: A Framework for Reconstructing Anti-Racist Institutions" (2018) 120(14) Teachers College Record 1.

[11]CE Matias, "'I Ain't Your Doc Student': The Overwhelming Presence of Whiteness and Pain at the Academic Neoplantation" in Kenneth Fasching-Varner and others (eds), *Racial Battle Fatigue in Higher Education: Exposing the Myth of Post-Racial America*(Rowman & Littlefield 2015) 60.

[12]https://blogs.kent.ac.uk/staff-student-news/2020/03/06/decolonial-walks/, post date, 6, March, 2020, accessed 3 June 2020.

[13]Matias (n 11) 60.

[14]Squire, Williams and Tuitt (n 10).

[15]Nadena Doharty, Manuel Madriaga and Remi Joseph-Salisbury, "The University Went to 'Decolonise' and All They Brought Back Was Lousy Diversity Double-Speak! Critical Race Counter-Stories from Faculty of Colour in 'Decolonial' Times" (2020) Educational Philosophy and Theory (forthcoming).

[16]Liz Morrish, "The Accident of Accessibility: How the Data of the TEF Creates Neoliberal Subjects" (2019) 33 Social Epistemology 355; Michael Tomlinson, Jürgen Enders and Rajani Naidoo, "The Teaching Excellence Framework: Symbolic Violence and the Measured Market in Higher Education" (2018) Critical Studies in Education (forthcoming).

[17]Robinson (n 19).

[18]Matias (n 11).

[19]In the same way Robinson (n 8) describes racial capitalism's logic already embedding a racialising logic in it before transatlantic slavery. Hence here, we are referring to both representation politics of "women", ie Athena swan and current conversations on "white working class" within the BME attainment gap.

I (Ahmed) as a junior faculty and graduate student along with other students like myself already perceive the institution with "mistrust". Everything that subsumes itself under hierarchy is part of the institution. Ultimately, all these formulations, i.e. policy and governance which guide the institution are, as David Gillborn describes these policies, "whiteness" performing itself.[20] As we discuss further below, "whiteness" is both ever present – looming, visible and subsuming the everyday life of students – yet it will not and cannot name itself for what it is and what it perpetrates – institutional racism.[21] In the UK HE sector, "decolonising" itself is continuing to be subsumed by this "plantation politics" especially when universities are signalling a call to "decolonise"[22] which Sara Ahmed has recently called "decolonial whiteness".[23] As Doharty, Madriaga and Joseph-Salisbury observe, "widespread calls to decolonize our universities have further embedded rather than dismantled whiteness".[24]

The Decolonise UoK project leads pre-empted these dynamics by being honest with the students about the gains and costs of attempting to disrupt the university's narrative. In a similar vein to what Squire, William and Tuitt refer to as "campus rebellions",[25] the project's aim was to form a "rebellion" which organically evolved into a space where the students led as "experts", (manifesto) knowledge producers and "owners" (stakeholders) within HE. However, the same conditions which alienate the students remain the ones which cause staff of colour to either participate in the "plantation politics" or be otherwise detrimentally affected by it. This is somewhat lost in presenting the manifesto as simply a product of "co-producing" research with students as experts.[26] What is not so explicit in the manifesto is how students trusted the staff to work with them to the extent they did and how a relationship was built between them. This relationship or student–staff relationality is a complex dynamic in which students felt "nurtured" which in turn led to the staff experiencing a sense of "healing".

3. *Building "trust" and student–staff relationality*

The symbiotic relation of student and teacher is also a personal one: specifically, what we experience and encounter in our everyday life. Our perception of what a scholar looks like, what authoritative knowledge looks like and where it comes from are all aspects of not just "geo and and body politics of knowledge"[27] but also in a visceral sense *how* we experience "knowledge" and "authority" through the everyday life of the university. The

[20]David Gillborn, "Education Policy as an Act of White Supremacy: Whiteness, Critical Race Theory and Education Reform" (2005) 20 Journal of Education Policy 485.

[21]Shirley Anne Tate and Paul Bagguley, "Building the Anti-Racist University: Next Steps" (2017) 20 Race Ethnicity and Education 289; Shirley Anne Tate and Damien Page, "Whiteliness and Institutional Racism: Hiding behind (Un)Conscious Bias" (2018) 13 Ethics and Education 141; R Shilliam, "Black Academia: The Doors Have Been Opened but the Architecture Remains the Same" in C Alexander and J Arday (eds), *Aiming Higher: Race, Inequality and Diversity in the Academy* (Runnymede Trust 2015) 32–34 <www.runnymedetrust.org/uploads/Aiming%20Higher.pdf>.

[22]Doharty, Madriaga and Joseph-Salisbury (n 15) 1.

[23]See tweet by Sara Ahmed, "Decolonial Whiteness Is No Less Occupying of Space as Colonial Whiteness" (@feministkilljoy) <https://twitter.com/saranahmed/status/1275350086734811139?s=21>.

[24]Doharty, Madriaga and Joseph-Salisbury (n 15) 1.

[25]Squire, Williams and Tuitt (n 10) 3.

[26]Dolores Delgado Bernal, "Critical Race Theory, Latino Critical Theory, and Critical Raced-Gendered Epistemologies: Recognizing Students of Color as Holders and Creators of Knowledge" (2002) 8 Qualitative Inquiry 105.

[27]Mignolo (n 7) 4.

manifesto itself refers to this through the need for a kaleidoscope hub for students and staff of colour as well as through support for staff of colour in their career progression.[28] This everyday experience is in *who* looks like "us" but also how knowledge, scholarship and *belonging* are reaffirmed through the breaking of whiteness as a universal norm. This has been particularly important to the project itself or any space of rebellion/resistance. In the very first meeting, students had the power to decide the project name in the context of other anti-racist student movements and decolonial and CRT literature. They were encouraged to question the premise of its aims and set the tone of its work. The project had many other moments where the barriers and walls built up by the institutionalised relationality were broken down – particularly in team meetings – where students and staff would discuss next steps of the project. In the capacity of a "student", I (Ahmed) saw a vast difference in the environment of the meetings. The expectation was already set by *how* the students saw Suhraiya; in a sense, there was already a particular mutual respect, honesty and level of trust established with the students. This was clearly reflected in how much "trust" was reciprocated by the staff to the students. The students were made to feel that their opinions were listened to but also crucially that they were essential and foundational to the project.

The act of listening to students and also putting them in the driving seat to co-produce knowledge that drew from their lived experiences was a form of resistance to institutional cultural practices. The "hidden" meetings, metrics, distance between staff came to be filled with trust from staff towards students. This trust has been reciprocal in that staff – who are academics – needed to let go of their own position of "knowing" what is best for the students. In short, the students are given a sense of dignity and respect where their growth is facilitated not "governed" through metrics. This is specifically important to build decolonial space as the intent of building a student–staff dynamic is to "democratise" the classroom. Staff who are committed to decolonial space would take an affective approach in building trust which is more than just about "content" but rather about creating an environment where "speaking" is not encumbered with preconditioned judgement on "intellect". This perception reflecting the conduct of staff is more than just looking opposite to the "white man" but means being in direct opposition to "whiteness" itself. That is precisely why "whiteness" understood as power[29] necessitates the building of an environment – the "democratisation"[30] of the classroom through "conduct" as a conscious act by staff.

In the project and our individual work[31] we emphasise this as a form of "conduct" and building an environment where it could be facilitated and developed through "principles". Inspired by other work with our collaborators like Building the Anti-Racist Classroom Collective, our suggestion to allies was to engage with the "principles" as a form of "practice".[32] This is articulated in the Kaleidoscope Network principles[33] which for us embody building a space and checking our intent/ethic before any action based

---

[28]Wahida and others (n 3).

[29]James Baldwin, *The Fire Next Time* (Vintage 2013).

[30]Delgado Bernal (n 26).

[31]Ahmed Raza Memon, "Decolonizing Research: Journey to the Research Ethics Forum" in Decolonise UoK Collective (n 2).

[32]This is distinct from a "safe space", and is closer to thinking of a space as an embodied interaction where intent and reflectiveness guide how we interact with others and ourselves within the space. It is recognising that there will be difficult conversations, mistakes, but we are guided by our "intent" and would reflect and act on our interaction.

[33]For the principles see <https://research.kent.ac.uk/sergj/wp-content/uploads/sites/486/2019/07/Kaleidoscope-Network-Principles-.pdf> accessed 21 June 2020.

on our understanding of whiteness in terms of power and privilege and what Fanon refers to as internalized colonialism.[34] For both the students and staff, developing trust has been underpinned by this set of practices to de-centre power, hierarchies and knowledge.

The academic pipeline is part of this building of a space since we see more barriers for researchers and students of colour becoming scholars within the academy where the main causes of a "broken" pipeline are structural racism and inequality.[35] The sense of not belonging and not being supported throughout their PhDs is also increasingly what causes emotional, psychological and mental difficulties amongst students of colour.[36] Part of the reason I (Ahmed) started the decolonising research collective was for this support for research students of colour with Dr Priya Hope and Dr Mo Afshary, which included a set of principles we wanted to follow as part of an ethic which was cognisant of these specific issues that researchers of colour face structurally in the UK academic system.[37] Building a decolonial space for students within the university through a student–staff dynamic is then also about building it all the way through the pipeline. The academic training to be a teacher often starts with the PhD training. What graduate students become is part of what they experience around them and through the reflection of "conduct" of mentors/teachers. This reflective imaging and seeing of a teacher acting a certain way, creating space and time is all also reflected in our image of a scholar. As a Muslim migrant scholar, my (Ahmed's) image of being a scholar is in my complete "self" not just in me being a PhD scholar in the research seminars but also in being a migrant Muslim.[38] Seeing scholars like myself, not just embracing but thinking through their subjectivity as a way to look at the world around them, was extremely important to me in my growth as a scholar. These everyday encounters i.e. conduct of mentors towards listening, respecting, reflecting even, my multiple levels of "self" is what develops that trust. Here then the question of what does a scholar look like, do they look like me, is not merely about the "colour of my skin", or a "fetishisation" of my "culture" but about the acceptance of all my "selves" as part of my existence and experience. More importantly, it is a sense of opposition to norms of "whiteness" perpetuated through the institution – that my "body" is finding a space to "heal" and "re-exist" beyond the exploitation by the university. In the life of the project, this was very sharply evident in terms of how teachers in particular but also students and those who are technically both displayed their trauma through different forms of affect: tears, silence, drawing, using the "principled" space to share that which we would not normally speak of.

Trust also comes at another register and Dr Akile Ahmet for example referred to "white allies" and understanding what that means to us.[39] It is important to look at "white" here again beyond just a biocentric and social understanding of racialisation, but in terms of power and privilege. It is important for us to be vigilant in these trusting

---

[34] Frantz Fanon, "Black Skin, White Masks" in *Social Theory Re-Wired: New Connections to Classical and Contemporary Perspectives* (2nd edn, Grove Press 2008).

[35] C Alexander and J Arday (eds), *Aiming Higher: Race, Inequality and Diversity in the Academy* (Runnymede Trust 2015); Deborah Gabriel and Shirley Anne Tate (eds), *Inside the Ivory Tower: Narratives of Women of Colour Surviving and Thriving in British Academia* (Trentham Books 2017); Paulette Williams and others, "The Broken Pipeline: Barrier to Black PhD Students Accessing Research Council Funding" (Leading Routes 2019).

[36] Jason Arday, "Exploring Black and Minority Ethnic (BME) Doctoral Students' Perceptions of a Career in Academia: Experiences, Perceptions and Career Progression" (University and College Union (UCU) 2017).

[37] Memon (n 31).

[38] ibid.

[39] BARC workshop Leeds Beckett (n 4).

relationships as they can become a trap since they are colonising the "decolonising" movement – in trying to "help".[40] Similar to understanding the university's commodification as a structure of racialisation perpetuated by the university, it is also important to question institutional "process" and the positionality of those perpetuating the processes of the colonial university.

In this sense it is also important to emphasise that creating a decolonial space does not do away with or erase structures of whiteness and the forms they take within the university space. Efforts against exclusionary behaviour have been and continue to be co-opted in neoliberal vocabularies such as "diversity", "multiculturalism", "internationalism", all of which are part of the university's institutional logics of whiteness.[41] Thus, as we have mentioned above, decolonisation – as a buzzword, co-opted by white academics and white allies – becomes and is part of the process whereby the university through its institutional logics rearranges ownership over power, knowledge and authority to maintain its "all subsuming" neoliberal position.[42] A decolonial space, however, becomes a rebellion against the white, colonial university. It is a place of disrupting power, hierarchy and authority, through the "healing" of staff and the growing consciousness of students *together* and not in separation. This allows for a decolonial space to then be a space of continuing resistance through re-existence rather than only struggling against colonial university logics ranging from silencing to co-optation.[43]

4. *"Courage" in the face of "whiteness"*

The relationality between students and staff built through *trust* has been contingent upon having a "decolonial" space to facilitate staff and students developing "courage" required for "campus rebellion". The condition of courage here is particularly inspired by Prof. Shirley Anne Tate's conceptualisation of *challenges* to building an anti-racist space.[44] "Challenge" here does not signify a hurdle per se but encompasses a broader range of steps, elements, characteristics of doing anti-racist work one needs to pay attention to when engaging with building an anti-racist space/community. Each letter of the "challenge" represents these elements:

> **"C"** is coping with fear of "whiteness" and overcoming it through the help of your community.
> **"H"** is holding on to hope and seeking help with the trauma of white hate.
> **"A"** denotes alliances that we must create and think about strategically, particularly when we ask what is required of the anti-racist white ally, what is required to be given up to be an ally or anti-racist.
> **"L"** signifies love or self-love as a radical potential for politics and re-existence.

---

[40] S Dar, A Dy and J Rodriguez, "Is Decolonising the New Black?" (2018) <www.leftofbrown.com/single-post/2018/07/12/Is-decolonising-the-new-black>.
[41] Sara Ahmed, "The Language of Diversity" (2007) 30 Ethnic and Racial Studies 235.
[42] Dar and others (n 40).
[43] See for example the statement of Decolonise UoK "The End" (2020) <https://decoloniseukc.org/2020/06/05/the-end/>.
[44] Shirley Anne Tate, "Where to From Here? – Final Thoughts" (Talk at Building the Anti-Racist Classroom Collective, Organising for Liberation Workshop, University of Leeds, 2019).

> "**L**" stands for liberation, more specifically liberating ourselves from mental slavery or internalised colonialism.
> "**E**" denotes engaging through loneliness as the process of this work despite the support around oneself can be "isolating". It leaves one feeling exposed, feeling as if you are alone in the department.
> "**N**" is negation or refusal as a conviction. It means to never see yourself living the trauma all over again and using that as a conviction for doing this work.
> "**G**" signifies giving trust – which also is a central theme in our own reflection in this article. Giving trust here is also with reference to earning trust from allies.
> "**E**" refers broadly to ethics of engagement with each other, ethics of care of self and of others and the relationality and interdependence of the two and which we explore as principles.

Courage then is about enacting this notion of *challenge* but not just as a result of necessity for students having to face the impact of "whiteness" around them as trust alone does not erase the structural racism/whiteness they will continue to experience whilst at university.[45] Courage is also important here given how decolonising work is likely to be co-opted by the neoliberal university, for its own benefit.[46] Here courage also becomes central in not knowing how and to what extent will the white colonial structures of the neoliberal university co-opt the efforts of building a decolonial space. However, it is also essential in continuing to keep the sanctity of the space and its intent which is a space for students/staff to re-exist, nourish, heal and grow with and through their community. The space provides them the courage to assert and reassert their dignity within white structures of power in the university.

Courage in a decolonial space is not just for students. Since the dynamic of staff–student relation is symbiotic in nature, the space created for such a relationality is also for the nourishment of all present in the space, including and especially the staff. As necessary as it is for staff of colour to be main facilitators that can create a trusting relation with students, they are also not recognised for the labour they put into doing the work.[47] As a number of scholars highlight it is often staff of colour that are given more "diversity" work and left to carry the emotional labour that comes with this work.[48] In our reflection then, it is important to point out how decolonial space should also be a space where staff can exercise their discretion in engaging/not engaging with the structures of the university since it is the staff who are in most direct contact with the bureaucratic machinations of whiteness in the neoliberal university.

A decolonial space often includes explanations of our traumas, descriptions of the violence we face and feel in order to just have a conversation about structural racism.

---

[45] Sadhvi Dar, "The Masque of Blackness: Or, Performing Assimilation in the White Academe" (2019) 26 Organization 432.

[46] ibid.

[47] Kalwant Bhopal, *White Privilege: The Myth of a Post-Racial Society* (Policy Press 2018); Sara Ahmed, *On Being Included* (Duke University Press 2012); Akwugo Emejulu and Leah Bassel, "Minority Women, Austerity and Activism" (2015) 57(2) Race and Class 86.

[48] Remi Joseph-Salisbury, "Institutionalised Whiteness, Racial Microaggressions and Black Bodies out of Place in Higher Education" (2019) 4 Whiteness and Education 1; Alexander and Arday (n 35); Jason Arday, "Being Black, Male and Academic: Navigating the White Academy" in Jason Arday and Heidi Safia Mirza (eds), *Dismantling Race in Higher Education: Racism, Whiteness and Decolonising the Academy* (Palgrave Macmillan 2018); Jason Arday, "Mental Health Issues of Black and Minority Ethnic Staff in Higher Education" in *Encyclopaedia of Teacher Education* (2020).

The institution itself becomes the place, as we have mentioned, of our bodily exploitation, appropriation and violence in the way we become "statistics" to sell – whether staff or students.[49] Through the university's own call to decolonisation, or equality/diversity these are translated to faculty of colour becoming "tokens" with the university hiding its neoliberal logics through "collecting" data on the "ethnic background" of the student body for recruitment drives. In the case of staff and students, equality policy, student success and now "decolonisation" agendas from the university translate to opening up of experiences of trauma, explanations of racialisation used to "individualise" people of colour rather than address systemic ways in which the institution perpetuates racism. This becomes a way to also reproduce the myth of a "race-neutral, meritocratic university" university[50] which hides how it operates to re-inscribe its neoliberal colonial logics.

Courage for us takes another form in the face of politics of the university. For example, in the BARC workshop,[51] an important point raised through discussion was the recounting of our battles within the university that can become a case of white students and staff consuming your trauma and vulnerability. Our hope is that a space which inculcates a dynamic of trust and nurturing between students and staff is a space that gives students the courage and support to assert their dignity. Through laborious "conduct" and building of a staff–student dynamic, encounters which develop trust and through a duty of care towards students, their trauma does not become a spectacle but acts as a call to care on part of those who are responsible for their care, namely, the staff. Prof. Shirley Anne Tate also refers to creating macro affirmations as being of utmost importance for building an anti-racist space.[52] At the same time, it is also important to be clear on how to create a "principled space" with values and specific requirements agreed upon and respected to create and sustain a decolonial space and an environment of care for students and staff in the face of pushback from whiteness.[53]

A decolonial space is at the centre about resisting/re-existing through the "cracks and fissures"[54] of the machinery. Within this space we also sustain our courage and grow consciousness along with students by relying on a lineage of teachers and scholars such as Bell Hooks, Gloria Anzaldúa, writers, activists and revolutionaries such as Audre Lorde, Ali Shariati, James Baldwin who become, as Karen Salt refers to them, our own "cannon".[55] Through the legacies and archives of these figures whose writing, words and actions stood in direct opposition to "whiteness" in all its myriad forms,[56] we see our own re-existence expressed in all forms as "courage" itself. This courage comes through "emoting" outside the vocabularies of the institution and the academy – which themselves can be just as alienating even when meant to be "critical".[57] As the Chicana

[49]Squire, Williams and Tuitt (n 10).

[50]Doharty, Madriaga and Joseph-Salisbury (n 15) 1.

[51]BARC workshop Leeds Beckett (n 4).

[52]Tate (n 44); this becomes even more important in the face of micro-aggressions that students of colour face in the university, for example see Joseph-Salisbury (n 48).

[53]See for example: <https://barcworkshop.org/resources/principled-space/> and <https://research.kent.ac.uk/sergj/wp-content/uploads/sites/486/2019/08/Chat-to-us.pdf>.

[54]Jivraj (n 5) 553.

[55]Dr Karen Salt, Talk at Decolonising University of Kent Conference (Decolonising the Curriculum Conference Playlist 2019) <https://research.kent.ac.uk/sergj/kaleidoscope-network-decolonising-the-university/>.

[56]Gilborn (n 20).

[57]Ahmed Raza Memon, "Pedagogy through Re-existence: Decolonizing as 'Doing' and Academic Responsibility" (*Decolonial Dialogues*, 2020) <https://decolonialdialogue.wordpress.com/2020/04/10/pedagogy-through-re-existence-decolonizing-as-doing-and-academic-responsibility/>.

feminist Gloria Anzaldúa says, her writing is meant to make the reader "feel" and her "being vulnerable", as well as expressing in different forms (art, dream, fiction), is an act of courage against the "coloniser".[58]

This courage to express in different forms is also part of consciousness of students and staff learning, reading and giving credit to international, transnational anti-imperial and anti-capitalist movements and their leaders throughout history. These include scholar leaders who paid particular attention to building solidarities across boundaries involved in their own decolonisation movements which were about more than just economy/territory. Also included are Malcolm X's efforts to build transnational solidarities across Asia, Africa,[59] Black Dubois's interaction with Dalit political leader B.R. Ambedkar,[60] amongst others who build and lead movements based on reassertion of dignity beyond academic/scholarly frames of knowing and being. Our idea of building decolonial space is a space which is conditioned – through principles – and building of a trust so that all forms of self-expression can flourish and come forward for the students to gain a sense of empowerment and dignity.

5. *Silence, "silencing" and discomfort in the heart of "whiteness"*

The violence of the silence, where there is no trust,

> Dims the light in your eyes, as your soul is trying to breathe,
> Where all these gazes around put you in mazes
> – and life is suddenly black and white
> You try to navigate a corridor of words and phrases,
> But the colour of your blood goes pale, and you swallow your truth as
> the silence and its violence is all you feel in your veins.

(Ahmed Raza Memon, Leeds BARC workshop, 2019)[61]

Another and perhaps the largest hurdle or fissure and more importantly goal in building a decolonial space is *silence* and the *breaking of silence*. Prof. Shirley Anne Tate, for example, reflects on this by asking us where the silence comes from.[62] It comes from not being valued – not being believed, feeling like you cannot say anything. What does it do to our students when they feel that we have no space? That is what silences students and teachers. It is already in the air, in the space we walk and breathe around us in the university – the hostile environment where you lose your pride with yourself and that is what silences you.

This silence or silencing is present in the everyday material, physical space around us[63] whether this is through buildings named after historical figures who were directly

[58] Gloria Anzaldúa, *The Gloria Anzaldúa Reader* (Duke University Press 2013).
[59] Seth M Markle, "Brother Malcolm, Comrade Babu: Black Internationalism and the Politics of Friendship" (2013) 36 Biography 540.
[60] Anindya Sekhar Purakayastha, "W.E.B. Du Bois, B.R. Ambedkar and the History of Afro-Dalit Solidarity" (2019) 6 Sanglap: Journal of Literary and Cultural Inquiry 20.
[61] Reflective poem written as part of BARC workshop Leeds Beckett (n 4).
[62] Tate (n 44).
[63] Caroline Howarth and Akile Ahmet, "'We Need to Speak About Race': Examining the Barriers to Full and Equal Participation in University Life" (*Impact of Social Sciences Blog*, 2016) <https://blogs.lse.ac.uk/impactofsocialsciences/2016/04/14/race-in-the-academy/> accessed 3 June 2020.

complicit with colonial violence and slavery[64] or in what is referred to as "canon" in our curriculum. As the manifesto and the project clearly demonstrated, students sense a form of being heard and not being listened to, of being seen and yet being ignored. The demands for a student/management forum to address violent racist episodes in the university, the demand for change in curriculum and most of all the demand for a dedicated space for further student–staff collaboration and mutual support, i.e. the Kaleidoscope Hub and Network[65] are all examples of this need for a place to be seen, heard and understood.

The manifesto then is a direct opposition to the silencing. The space that was created through the project became the space for students to break their silences and to have the courage to continue to fight through the "silencing" from the institution through its responses. The institutional response itself is a constant distancing of those that speak up and also is reflective of what it already embeds within the university student body – that the students have no intrinsic potential and value unless these are "produced" through the transaction of a "university education as service". The structure of the university and the institutionalised hierarchies as well as bureaucracies it creates to distance students are what create the "silencing".

Throughout these themes we have identified and particularly on silence and silencing, "discomfort" remains a constant lingering affective element. This discomfort becomes evident as part of structural and micro responses to conversations on race.[66] The sub-discipline of critical whiteness studies speaks to and about these emergent conversations on the responses to "discomfort", "denial", "hesitance" and "white guilt".-[67] "Discomfort" here, for us in our reflection is not a pedagogical response to conversations on race within and outside the academy,[68] but a necessary element of the "decolonising" process and the creation of an anti-racist space. It is a material reality which has to be part of conversations surrounding violence we face, we perpetrate and have to tackle regardless of our positionality. In building decolonial space, students and staff of colour have to be in a constant state of "discomfort" which is part of speaking out in courage and breaking the silence. It remains a continuous element of our efforts in speaking to, about and against "whiteness" as a form of neoliberal, capitalist structure, as a form of power and as a performance. However, it is also rendered invisible through a shift on the "discomfort" of "whiteness" responding to conversation on race.

In reflecting on the conditions for creating decolonial space, we therefore question the extent to which the shift on white "discomfort" becomes yet again a performance of whiteness and thus just another form of *silencing*. White discomfort, like white ally-ship, becomes just another part of institutional logics reiterating racial capitalist structures of the university through micro-interactions. Not only does discomfort become a discourse of intellectual/academic capital[69] for critical whiteness studies, it also relegates the inherent

---

[64]Anamika Misra, "Decolonising the Canon of Keynes" (2020) in Decolonise UoK Collective (n 2).
[65]Wahida and others (n 3).
[66]For the relevant literature see for example, Robin DiAngelo, "White Fragility: Why It's So Hard to Talk to White People About Racism" (The Good Men Project 2015); Gloria Wekker, *White Innocence* (Duke University Press 2016).
[67]N Aveling, "Critical Whiteness Studies and the Challenges of Learning to Be a 'White Ally'" (2005) Borderlands E-journal <https://researchrepository.murdoch.edu.au/id/eprint/8494/>.
[68]Michalinos Zembylas, "Affect, Race, and White Discomfort in Schooling: Decolonial Strategies for 'Pedagogies of Discomfort'" (2018) 13 Ethics and Education 86.
[69]Sara Ahmed, "A Phenomenology of Whiteness" (2007) 8 Feminist Theory 149.

and necessary nature of discomfort of decolonising work on people of colour who continue to put themselves in the space of vulnerability and "trauma consumption".[70]

6. *Conclusion*

This article reflects on not just establishing the potential/importance of a decolonial space but more so on the conditions required of building such a space. In the specific context of Decolonise UoK the conditions of a decolonial space include student–staff relationality built on *trust, courage* and understanding of the different role and impact of *silencing/silence*. These factors are even more important, as "decolonising"/"anti-racism" and other measures can become subsumed and incorporated within the institution to perpetuate its colonial neoliberal logics rather than address or dismantle them. Any decolonial space based on student–staff relationality then becomes a "crack and fissure" for resistance[71] but also a way to "choke the consumption by the university"[72] and its colonial neoliberal logics.

It is in this way we understand a decolonial space as a "campus rebellion", a place for resistance through re-existence. Beyond just a form of resistance,[73] this re-existence is also a form of constant growing and evolving without knowing what the outcome will be as part of the resistance. "Not knowing" is, in this instance, a state of mind in understanding our relationship to our lived experiences in order to heal and grow.To "not know" what the "end" of decolonised university looks like is an acceptance of an "unknown" not as a matter of pessimism or nihilistic defeat but as a process of finding new horizons of love, existence and dignity. Thus, while we emphasise how decolonisation is a "process",[74] we have also shown through this article/and the collective project why it is worth thinking about the ethics of the process. It is also crucial to understand how we embody the idea of a "process" without an end in different forms in our everyday praxis. We contend that in decolonising beyond just a process or as form of re-existence, it is also essential to think about the ethics of the process and continuous re-existence, given how we must place ourselves in constant opposition to "whiteness" as a form of power wherever it may emerge from. In the end, after all, *we* are also part of the colonial neoliberal institution.

Disclosure statement

No potential conflict of interest was reported by the authors.

ORCID

Ahmed Raza Memon http://orcid.org/0000-0002-3502-7743
Suhraiya Jivraj http://orcid.org/0000-0002-1371-3806

---

[70]BARC workshop Leeds Beckett (n 4).
[71]Jivraj (n 5) 553.
[72]George Yancy, "A Letter of Love: An Encounter with White Backlash" (Keynote, Third Building the Anti-Racist Classroom Workshop at Queen Mary University, 2019).
[73]Akwugo Emejulu and Francesca Sobande, "Introduction" in *To Exist Is to Resist* (Pluto Press 2019).
[74]Gurminder K Bhambra, Dalia Gebrial and Kerem Nişancıoğlu, "Introduction: Decolonising the University?" in *Decolonising the University* (Pluto Press 2018).

"Law", "order", "justice", "crime": disrupting key concepts in criminology through the study of colonial history

J.M. Moore

ABSTRACT

This article reviews a final year undergraduate module, "Crime, Punishment and Justice in the British Empire", evaluating the extent to which it contributed a de/postcolonial perspective within the delivery of a criminology programme's curriculum. To do this the paper first critiques the discipline of criminology and its links with colonialism, before describing how this module was designed to address criminology's "colonial problem". The paper then explores the design and delivery of the module from the perspective of the author before providing a student perspective on the module based on data collected through five semi-structured interviews. The paper concludes that although the module largely met its objectives, a single option module can only have a limited impact. If criminology can be decolonised (something the paper remains agnostic about) it will require a radical rethinking of the curriculum at a programme level.

Introduction

This paper explores the author's experience of designing and delivering a final year undergraduate module "Crime, Punishment and Justice in the British Empire", in the first semester of the 2018/2019 academic year. The module was delivered at Newman University, Birmingham, a small university whose students are drawn almost exclusively from local working-class communities.[1] It was offered as an option on the BA Criminology programme and designed to allow students to explore concepts central to the wider programme such as law, order, justice, "crime" and punishment through an engagement with the history of the British empire. Whilst traditional histories of "crime", criminal law, and punishment draw exclusively from the metropole – normally in a Whiggish manner that portrays them as stories of the progress of civilisation – a global perspective, highlighting both pre-colonial indigenous traditions[2] and the ways that European states utilised criminal law in the governance of their colonies, has the potential to unsettle and disrupt a criminology student's understanding of criminal law.

---

[1]The University's 2019 Transparency return shows that 54% of the university's student intake was in the EIMD (English Index of Multiple Deprivation) Quartile 1 (the most "deprived" quartile) and that 47% of students were classified as "BAME". (The dataset [Table 1b] can be accessed via <www.newman.ac.uk/knowledge-base/applications-offers-acceptances-and-registrations-2018-19-entrants/>.)

[2]Although the author strongly supports the inclusion of such traditions in the curriculum, this was not attempted within the module analysed in this paper.

The module was intended to meet four key objectives. First, to use the history of the British empire to critique key criminological concepts. Secondly, to use colonial history to explore the role of racism and "race" in criminal law and criminal justice practice. Thirdly, to explore the significance of the state, its deployment of penal law as a governance strategy and its use of "emergencies" to justify exceptionalism. Finally, it was intended to contribute to the provision of a curriculum that had relevance for all students. The module's theoretical focus was therefore on the concepts of "crime" and "race", which could then be explored through a selection of case studies drawn from the wider history of the British empire. Thirteen out of a cohort of 27 chose to take the module. The relatively small size of the programme meant the students all knew each other well and they had an established relationship with me. Although all the students had been born in England many of their grandparents had been born in places that had been colonised by Britain, namely, Pakistan, India, Jamaica and Ireland.

This article sets out, first, to explore the discipline of criminology and why a (post/de) colonial perspective is particularly relevant for the subject's curriculum in higher education. It does this in two sections: first, a brief critique of the "problems" – from a decolonial perspective – of the discipline of criminology and secondly, by setting out how this module was designed to address these problems and disrupt the key concepts that ground the discipline. The article then moves on to an evaluation of the module, in terms of both its design and its delivery. This analysis is informed by five semi-structured interviews of students who took the module undertaken by the researcher.[3] The paper concludes that whilst this module provided students with valuable (post/de)colonial perspectives on key criminal law concepts it was no substitute for decolonising the wider curriculum.

The problems with criminology

At this time colonialism's significance to education is being recognised and all disciplines are being challenged to "decolonise".[4] Disciplines emerged in Europe at the same time as it developed power/knowledge/difference to govern both its capitalist metropole and its colonies.[5] Like other disciplines, criminology's "historical emergence … was occasioned by a problem, a requirement, an obstacle of a theoretical or practical order".[6] That order was the capitalist and imperial order. In fulfilling this function criminology has always been "entirely utilitarian".[7] For Michel Foucault, criminology "is of such utility … that it does not even need to seek a theoretical justification for itself".[8] As a discipline criminology is unique in that its subject matter – "crime" – is determined by the state. Given that it is the state that determines criminology's subject matter, it is concerning that the discipline generates theories that often "have no concept or theory of the state".[9] As a consequence the discipline tends to ignore the often oppressive and violent nature of the state itself. Given the state's central role not

[3]Ethical approval was granted for this research by the Research Ethics Committee of Newman University #S2018/035.
[4]Gurminder K Bhambra, Dalia Gebrial and Kerem Nişancioğlu (eds), *Decolonising the University* (Pluto Press 2018).
[5]Stuart Hall, *The Fateful Triangle: Race, Ethnicity, Nation* (Harvard University Press 2017).
[6]Michel Foucault, *The Order of Things* (Routledge 2002) 376.
[7]Michel Foucault, *Power/Knowledge: Selected Interviews and Other Writings 1972-1977* (Harvester Wheatsheaf 1980) 47.
[8]ibid.
[9]Stuart Hall and others, *Policing the Crisis: Mugging, the State, and Law and Order* (Macmillan Press 1978) 190.

only in defining "crime", but also in responding to it through penal law and its criminal justice agencies, it is vital for criminology to understand how the modern state, in the metropole, settler colonies and the post-colonial "independent" states has been shaped not only by capitalism, but by the challenges of colonial governance.[10]

Whilst the focus on "crime" ensures criminology's range is determined by the state, "crime" existed before, and without, criminology. Criminology's specific contribution was its invention of the criminal; "crime" became something committed not by otherwise normal people but by the criminal "other".[11] The penal philosophy of Bentham had perceived criminals as rational beings, motivated by exactly the same forces and influences as everybody else.[12] The key to stopping, or at least minimising, offences was to ensure the certainty of receiving an appropriate punishment.[13] Criminology changed this. During the nineteenth century criminals ceased to be rational beings, they became both morally defective and in need of reformation. Lombroso, and other early criminologists, discovered the "born criminal": an incurable primitive being, subhuman, and entirely unlike the "normal" person.[14] Criminology invented "an enemy mysterious, unrecognized by history ... the CRIMINAL".[15] So why was it that, in the nineteenth century, this "mysterious" and "unrecognized" criminal was able to be perceived? In the preceding centuries Europe had been engaged in invasion, genocide, slavery, asset stripping and a myriad of other oppressive and exploitative activities across the globe.[16] Colonial domination required humanity to *not* be universal. Invented in the metropole and deployed in the colony, "race" (or more accurately racism) enabled the creation of the "racial other", the subject without the rights and liberty of the liberal "white" citizen.[17] The discipline most central to the project of scientifically proving the otherness of the colonial subject was anthropology and Lombroso chose to initially brand the discipline that would become criminology as "criminal anthropology".[18] When in 1924 the Indian legal scholar K.S. Pillai observed that: "The wholly-haired African Negro reminds us of several characteristics of Lombroso's born criminal ... " (p. 136) his association was no coincidence. Lombroso's "other", the born criminal, could only be discovered because of the racial "other", anthropology's invention legitimising colonialism.[19]

These issues are almost exclusively avoided in the teaching of criminology. "Crime" is largely presented as an unproblematic concept, with criminal justice institutions and the operation of penal law accepted as its natural responses. My own research, seeking to explain contemporary levels of penality in the metropole through historical analysis, led me to move beyond the metropole and to a focus on colonial governance. Whilst the punitive turn of recent decades could *not* be explained by a historic focus on Britain, a wider perspective of the penality of the British state, in its empire, showed clear

---

[10]Partha Chatterjee, *The Black Hole of Empire: History of a Global Practice of Power* (Princeton University Press 2012).

[11]David Garland, *Punishment and Welfare: A History of Penal Strategies* (Gower 1985).

[12]Jeremy Bentham, "Principles of Penal Law" in John Bowring (ed), *The Works of Jeremy Bentham*, Volume I (William Tait 1843) 365–80.

[13]ibid.

[14]Cesare Lombroso, *Criminal Man* (Mary Gibson and Nicole Hahn Rafter trs, Duke University Press 2006).

[15]Raffaele Garofalo, *Criminology* (Little, Brown, and Company 1914) xxvii. Emphasis in the original.

[16]Aimé Césaire, *Discourse on Colonialism* (Joan Pinkham tr, Monthly Review Press 2000).

[17]Uday Singh Mehta, *Liberalism and Empire: A Study in Nineteenth-Century British Liberal Thought* (2nd edn, University of Chicago Press 1999); Domenico Losurdo, *Liberalism: A Counter-History* (Verso 2011).

[18]Nicole Hahn Rafter, *Creating Born Criminals* (University of Illinois Press 1997).

[19]KS Pillai, *Principles of Criminology: The Tagore Law Lectures – 1920* (Vest & Co 1924).

continuities.[20] The introduction of this history makes the progressive and civilising Whig accounts of the development of criminal justice unsustainable. Criminology's link to "crime" makes attempts to engage with colonialism problematic. For example, when Emmanuel Onyeozili claims that the British occupation of Lagos was "international terrorism and a violation of international law" and Biko Agozino argues that the "enslavement of Africans was a crime against humanity" they fail to acknowledge that however harmful, vile and repugnant the behaviours of British colonialism were, they were not crimes.[21] Indeed, the British state carefully deployed law to legitimise its conduct. Rather than being "crimes" these abuses of human rights show the limitation of the concept and the need to seek explanations and counter-colonial praxis which recognise the limitations of criminology's core concepts. "Law", "order", "justice", "crime" – concepts often presented as unproblematic in the curriculum of criminology – become much more challenging when explored through the history of the *legal* enslavement of Africans, the *legal* genocide of indigenous peoples, the *legal* looting of India, the racist colonial *legal* codes, and the wide range of other *legalised* (and *legally* enforced) injustices and harms that characterised colonial governance. Without this history any study of "crime", criminals or the criminal justice system is not only incomplete but fundamentally inaccurate.

Explaining how criminology "continues to operate largely as a repressive technology", Agozino has highlighted how it "was developed primarily as a tool for imperialist domination".[22] Indeed Agozino has repeatedly drawn attention to the highly problematic relationship between criminology and colonialism observing that criminologists have "completely ignored the crimes of colonialism and the epochal struggles for decolonisation while focusing on street crimes".[23] Criminology therefore has a colonial problem.[24] It not only has, like all disciplines, to confront the colonial legacy of the academy and the states in which it seeks to operate, but through its focus on "crime", it has accepted that the state defines its remit. Its foundational contribution, the invention of the criminal "other", a development made possible through the utilising of the racist concept of the racial "other" makes decolonisation even more difficult. Current attempts to decolonise the discipline are problematic. For example, Southern Criminology, which explicitly states that is not intended "to dismiss the conceptual and empirical advances in criminology, but to more usefully de-colonize and democratize the toolbox of available criminological concepts, theories and methods", adopts a largely geographic conception of "Southern".[25] This has enabled settler colonies and their criminological discourse to be located in the "South" thereby failing to recognise that, as Edouard Glissant has pointed out, "(t)he west is not in the west. It is a project, not a place."[26] Likewise, recent Australian

[20]JM Moore, "Is the Empire Coming Home? Liberalism, Exclusion and the Punitiveness of the British State" (2014) 14 Papers from the British Criminology Conference 31.

[21]Emmanuel C Onyeozili, "Gunboat Criminology and the Colonization of Africa" in Anita Kalunta-Crumpton and Biko Agozino (eds), *Pan-African Issues in Crime and Justice* (Ashgate 2004) 225; Biko Agozino, "Reparative Justice: A Pan-African Criminology Primer" in Anita Kalunta-Crumpton and Biko Agozino (eds), *Pan-African Issues in Crime and Justice* (Ashgate 2004) 234.

[22]Biko Agozino, *Counter-Colonial Criminology: A Critique of Imperialist Reason* (Pluto Press 2003) 228.

[23]Biko Agozino, "The Withering Away of the Law: An Indigenous Perspective on the Decolonisation of the Criminal Justice System and Criminology" (2018) 3(1) Journal of Global Indigeneity, Article 2, 6.

[24]Space does not permit me to further develop this point. However, it is important to stress that this "problem" presents in very different ways in independent former colonies, settler-colonies and the metropole.

[25]Kerry Carrington, Russell Hogg and Máximo Sozzo, "Southern Criminology" (2016) 56 British Journal of Criminology 1.

[26]Edouard Glissant, *Caribbean Discourse: Selected Essays* (University of Virginia Press 1992) 2.

attempts at Decolonising Criminology and introducing Indigenous Criminology have failed to engage fully with the genocidal logic of settler colonialism.[27] To date these new paradigms have failed to satisfactorily demonstrate whether criminology, an "imperialistic discipline", can be decolonised.[28]

Crime, punishment and justice in the British empire – the curriculum

Designing the curriculum for a one semester module is always challenging. This is particularly the case with one covering a broad topic with a wide geographic and historic span. The starting point was to identify key theoretical concepts required to underpin the module. The two selected were "crime" and "race". These were to be used to explore the case studies that formed the bulk of the module and were central to the assignments. A range of potential case studies were identified and two were selected before the module ran, one focused on slavery ("Not a Crime? The Atlantic Trade in Enslaved Africans") and the other on the economic exploitation of India ("Robbery with Violence – the Mugging of India"). From a range of further case studies suggested by me, students selected to explore: the genocide of Australia's indigenous peoples; the Morant Bay uprising in Jamaica; and the Mau Mau uprising in Kenya. In addition, there was an introductory session on the wider history of the British empire, a visit to the International Slavery Museum in Liverpool and a concluding session exploring the relevance of the module to contemporary criminal justice in Britain today.

Whilst the student cohort were familiar with the fragility of the concept of "crime" from a previous module, this module provided an opportunity to utilise the history of colonial penality to re-engage critically with the attempts of scholars to develop, for criminology, a viable definition of "crime". "Crime" would appear, at first sight, to be simply an act or omission proscribed by the criminal law. As such it includes acts that are not only widespread but committed regularly by the majority of the population. "Crime" is widespread, mundane, ordinary behaviour that is potentially "in endless supply".[29] However, for a discipline whose raison d'être is its identification of the criminal "other", such a definition is unacceptable. Attempting to narrow the discipline's focus, Paul Tappan argued that "(o)nly those ...who have been adjudicated as such by the courts" are criminals.[30] Whilst convenient, such a definition wilfully ignores questions about who makes the law, what motivates them, how the law is enforced (or not), and the clear evidence of differential treatment, in particular on the basis of class and race, which characterises criminal justice practice.[31] Ultimately a focus on a legalistic definition leads to the conclusion that "the criminal law is the formal cause of crime".[32]

To escape this conclusion, criminologists have sought to develop definitions of "crime" independent of criminal law. Raffaele Garofalo deployed the concept of "*natural*

---

[27]Harry Blagg and Thalia Anthony, *Decolonising Criminology: Imagining Justice in a Postcolonial World* (Palgrave Macmillan 2019); Chris Cunneen and Juan Tauri, *Indigenous Criminology* (Policy Press 2016).

[28]Biko Agozino, "Reparative Justice: A Pan-African Criminology Primer" in Anita Kalunta-Crumpton and Biko Agozino (eds), *Pan-African Issues in Crime and Justice* (Ashgate 2004) 228.

[29]Nils Christie, *A Suitable Amount of Crime* (Routledge 2004) 10.

[30]Paul W Tappan, "Who Is the Criminal?" (1947) 12 American Sociological Review 96, 100.

[31]William J Chambliss and Milton Mankoff (eds), *Whose Law? What Order? A Conflict Approach to Criminology* (Wiley 1976).

[32]Jerome Michael and Mortimer Adler, *Crime, Law and Social Science* (Harcourt, Brace 1933) 5.

crime" which he defined as "those acts which no civilized society can refuse to recognize as criminal and repress by means of punishment".[33] To give credibility to the concept of the criminal, Garofalo argued for a division of currently criminal offences into "natural crimes" and "mere transgressions", asking his readers:

> what is to prevent the existence, side by side with the criminal code, of a separate code of disobediences, the one dealing with natural criminality, the other with all mere transgressions of law which public policy finds it necessary to repress with measures of severity?[34]

Some criminologists have argued for a focus on human rights, utilising the UN's 1948 Universal Declaration of Human Rights in theorising state crime.[35] Others have adopted a human rights approach that extends well beyond the UN Declaration with, for example, Herman and Julia Schwendinger arguing that "imperialism, racism, sexism and poverty" should be considered crimes.[36] Other criminologists have argued that the focus should be on perceiving "crime" as ideological censure, as anti-social behaviour, or historical invention whilst others have argued that rather than concentrate on "crime" the focus should be on harm or deviance. The module was intended to allow students to revisit this criminological theory, but this time to interrogate it through its application in a number of colonial case studies.

The student cohort at the start of the module had a very individualistic understanding of racism, largely based on their own, their families' and their friends' experiences in contemporary Birmingham. To engage with the module's case studies, it was necessary for students to develop an understanding of how structural racism was deployed by elites to facilitate the governance of empire.[37] The societies colonialism created were inherently racist and understanding how penal law functioned within colonial spaces required students to explore how this racism operated. "Race" was central to colonial law and justice and as Bal Tilack, the radical Indian nationalist, observed ironically in 1907, the "goddess of British Justice, though blind, is able to distinguish unmistakably black from white".[38]

Teaching the module as a white man from a privileged position, and with a personal history connected to the legacy of empire,[39] I felt it inappropriate to lecture my students about "race", when, for so many of them, it was a lived experience. Therefore, in approaching "race", the starting point was the students' own understandings and their experiences of racism. From this foundation, students were asked to engage with two contemporary authors' autobiographical accounts of their experiences of racism and how they had attempted to place their individual experiences in the historic context of the structural racism of the British empire.[40] These accounts provided the bridge from which we could move from students' individual experiences

---

[33] Raffaele Garofalo, *Criminology* (Little, Brown, and Company 1914) 4, 5. Emphasis in the original.

[34] ibid 59.

[35] Stanley Cohen, "Human Rights and Crimes of the State: The Culture of Denial" (1993) 26 Australian & New Zealand Journal of Criminology 97.

[36] Herman and Julia Schwendinger, "Defenders of Order or Guardians of Human Rights?" in Ian Taylor, Paul Walton and Jock Young (eds), *Critical Criminology* (Routledge & Kegan Paul 1975) 148.

[37] Patrick Wolfe, *Traces of History: Elementary Structures of Race* (Verso 2016).

[38] Cited in Elizabeth Kolsky, *Colonial Justice in British India: White Violence and the Rule of Law* (Cambridge University Press 2010) 4.

[39] My childhood was largely spent in former British colonies where my father was posted by the British Foreign and Commonwealth Office.

[40] Akala, *Natives: Race and Class in the Ruins of Empire* (Two Roads 2018); Reni Eddo-Lodge, *Why I'm No Longer Talking to White People About Race* (Bloomsbury 2018).

to exploring the theoretical literature on "race" and racism. This was introduced initially through videos: Stuart Hall talking about "race" as a floating signifier and Patrick Wolfe's comparison of colonial and racial regimes.[41] Watching these as a class meant that discussions could both focus on understanding Hall and Wolfe's arguments and relating them back to both students' own lived experiences and the central role of "race" to colonialism.

The first case study considered by the class was "Not a Crime? The Atlantic Trade in Enslaved Africans". Our starting point was the legality of chattel slavery in the Americas and the challenge this presents to us as criminologists. This topic was also introduced through videos, with the students watching episode two of David Olusoga's documentary *Black and British: A Forgotten History*, to provide an introduction to the scale and nature of the Atlantic Trade in enslaved Africans as well as highlight Britain's central role in it.[42] The second video was the interactive *The Atlantic Slave Trade in Two Minutes* which we watched and interacted with in class.[43] This graphically illustrated the sheer scale of the enterprise and by freezing it at various points we were able to click on any of the multitude of dots – all of which represented a crossing – and identify individual ships, their nationality and the number of enslaved Africans they transported. This provided a powerful tool for identifying Britain's central role in the business. I have deliberately used words like "enterprise" and "business" in this article, as I did in the class, to stress the commercial nature of the trade in enslaved Africans and throughout the session, I continued to emphasise its centrality to the economies of Europe and the Americas. In particular we looked at the wealth it created for Britain. The students, unsurprisingly, regarded the trade as a "crime against humanity". Whilst it was, it was not a "crime" in law and this required us to consider, however abhorrent we may have found it, what its legality (and the vigorous protection the law gave it) says about key concepts such as the law, "crime", criminals and justice and how this has an impact on us as criminologists. For those students interested in further independent study it was suggested they watch the other three episodes of *Black and British* and/or read the excellent accompanying book.[44]

Our second case study was "Robbery with Violence – the Mugging of India". Prior to the class students read the first chapter of Shashi Tharoor's *Inglorious Empire*.[45] In exploring the chapter, we went back to the concept of "crime" and the assumptions of criminology. The stereotypical robber is either an individual of low economic status, often Black, or possibly organised into a "gang" or the Mafia. The Crown Prosecution Service (CPS) website defines robbery as an offence "committed when a *person* steals and immediately before or at the time of doing so, and in order to do so, he uses force on any person, or puts or seeks to put any person in fear of being then and there subject to force".[46] This definition provided a basis for evaluating the conduct of first the East India Company and secondly the British state. Whilst we did, briefly, engage with

---

[41]"Race, the Floating Signifier: Featuring Stuart Hall" (*YouTube*) <https://youtu.be/bMo2uiRAf30> accessed 26 October 2019; "Patrick Wolfe – Comparing Colonial and Racial Regimes" (*YouTube*) <https://youtu.be/xwj5bcLG8ic> accessed 26 October 2019.

[42]"Freedom", Episode 2 of *Black and British: A Forgotten History* (BBC 2 Television, 16 November 2016).

[43]Slate, *The Atlantic Slave Trade in Two Minutes* <www.slate.com/articles/life/the_history_of_american_slavery/2015/06/animated_interactive_of_the_history_of_the_atlantic_slave_trade.html> accessed 29 October 2019.

[44]David Olusoga, *Black and British: A Forgotten History* (Macmillan 2016).

[45]Shashi Tharoor, *Inglorious Empire: What the British Did to India* (Penguin 2016).

[46]CPS, "Theft Acts" <www.cps.gov.uk/legal-guidance/theft-act-offences> accessed 29 October 2019.

apologists for British imperialism,[47] the history of British India demonstrated how powerful corporate actors and the state can engage in large-scale robbery. Despite it being robbery, on a grand scale, we explored how these powerful interests used law, the concept of "crime" and the power to punish to legitimise their harmful behaviours. Although this seminar had intended to focus on exploring economic exploitation, the students were extremely interested in the wider history of the sub-continent. In particular a number, whose families had Pakistani heritage, wanted to know more about Partition, a key legacy of colonialism. Several students subsequently researched the topic in some depth independently.

The next case study was "Genocide: The Experience of Australia's Indigenous Peoples". In preparation students were asked to watch John Pilger's film, *Utopia*.[48] This was chosen because I wanted the class to explore not only how British settlement of what is now known as Australia affected the continent's indigenous peoples, but also how this affects Aborigines' experience of criminal justice today. The United Nations (UN) defines genocide as:

> ... any of the following acts committed with intent to destroy, in whole or in part, a national, ethnical, racial or religious group, as such:
>
> 1. Killing members of the group;
> 2. Causing serious bodily or mental harm to members of the group;
> 3. Deliberately inflicting on the group conditions of life calculated to bring about its physical destruction in whole or in part;
> 4. Imposing measures intended to prevent births within the group;
> 5. Forcibly transferring children of the group to another group.[49]

In the class we looked at how the colonisation of Australia fell within the UN's definition and explored how the criminal law was written and enforced (or not) to facilitate this genocide. We explored how racism and concepts of "race" were utilised to justify genocidal policies and discussed the ways these ideas continue to influence both criminal justice policy and practice. We explored an interactive map of frontier massacres from the late eighteenth to the early twentieth centuries.[50] We also looked at the massive over-targeting and over-representation of indigenous peoples in the criminal justice systems of Australia and other settler colonies today.

The next unit was entitled "(Dis)order & (In)justice I – Morant Bay, Jamaica, 1865". In preparation students were asked to watch a brief film and read a short article.[51] From

[47] For example, Adrian Lee, "The Remarkable Raj: Why Britain Should Be Proud of Its Rule in India" (*Daily Express Online*, 22 June 2013) <www.express.co.uk/news/uk/409374/The-Remarkable-Raj-Why-Britain-should-be-proud-of-its-rule-in-India> accessed 29 October 2019.

[48] *Utopia* [Online] John Pilger, Australia, (Network Releasing, 2013) <http://johnpilger.com/videos/utopia> accessed 29 October 2019. The film is long, nearly two hours and only about a half watched it to the end.

[49] United Nations, "Genocide" <www.un.org/en/genocideprevention/genocide.shtml> accessed 29 October 2019.

[50] Centre for 21st Century Humanities, "Colonial Frontier Massacres in Central and Eastern Australia, 1780-1930" (*University of Newcastle*) <https://c21ch.newcastle.edu.au/colonialmassacres/map.php> accessed 16 October 2020.

[51] IMJamaica, "Morant Bay Rebellion – History Uncovered" <https://youtu.be/BEH7fBz4K00> (accessed 29 October 2019); Jake Cavanaugh, "The Cause of the Morant Bay Rebellion: 1865" (University of Miami Digital Collections, University of Miami) <http://scholar.library.miami.edu/emancipation/jamaica4.htm> accessed 29 October 2019.

the start of this workshop it was clear that the students were struggling to contextualise Morant Bay. This required a brief review of the history of the island, its colonisation; the genocide of its indigenous population (which linked back to the previous class); the introduction of large-scale cultivation of sugar cane and the resultant introduction of indentured Irish, Welsh and English labour, and subsequently, on a far greater scale, enslaved Africans. We then discussed the history of the resistance of enslaved Africans, including the 1831 Baptist War, and how the institution of slavery was maintained through both brutality and the construction of a legal framework empowering whites to maintain their dominance through legalised violence. The role of resistance in the abolition of slavery was explored. We then discussed post-emancipation Jamaican society, and how it remained unequal and fundamentally unjust and how the emancipated Black population continued to face discrimination, exclusion from political power and poverty. It was this injustice and the frustration of attempts to raise the Black population's grievances through official channels that provided the background to Morant Bay.[52] This exploration of the Island's history prior to 1865 took up most of the class and highlighted that I had presumed far too much prior knowledge. As a result of this discussion we resolved as a class to visit the International Slavery Museum in Liverpool. This visit took place a fortnight later.

The visit to the International Slavery Museum in Liverpool occurred in the ninth of the 12 weeks of the module. The trip provided an additional way for students to learn about the subject and an opportunity for conversations during the four hours we spent on the train. At this point students were working on their essays and it was particularly productive to talk about these in small groups. The experience of the visit was very positive and complemented the videos and readings we were using on the module. A further unit exploring the resistance of the colonised and the response of the British state, "(Dis)order and (In)justice II – Torture, Concentration Camps and the Noose in Kenya, 1952–1960", had to be cancelled for personal reasons.

The final workshop was entitled: "Crime, Punishment and Justice in the British Empire: What Is the Relevance Today?" Students were asked to return to the Akala book to read the chapter "Police, Peers and Teenage Years" and a paper I had written "Is the Empire Coming Home?".[53] The module, although historic, was intended to enable students to explore key criminological concepts and this session allowed students to relate the relevance of the historic content to contemporary criminal justice practice. Akala's experiences as a Black boy could be linked to his analysis earlier in the book of colonialism. Evidence of the difference between those young men committing violent offences (predominately white) and those being identified by the police as gang members (predominately Black) suggested that the racism utilised in the governance of colonial populations directly shapes contemporary policing perceptions.[54] Akala's experiences were replicated by class members and their family and friends' experiences which suggests that the spirit of colonialism lives on in the stereotype of who is (and

[52]David Olusoga, *Black and British: A Forgotten History* (Macmillan: Oxford University Press 2016).

[53]Akala, *Natives: Race and Class in the Ruins of Empire* (Two Roads 2018). A number of students had read the full book by this stage of the module; JM Moore, "Is the Empire Coming Home? Liberalism, Exclusion and the Punitiveness of the British State" (2014) 14 Papers from the British Criminology Conference <http://britsoccrim.org/volume14/pbcc_2014_moore.pdf> accessed 26 October 2019.

[54]Patrick Williams and Becky Clarke, *Dangerous Associations: Joint Enterprise, Gangs and Racism* (Centre for Crime and Justice Studies 2016) <www.crimeandjustice.org.uk/publications/dangerous-associations-joint-enterprise-gangs-and-racism> accessed 29 October 2019.

isn't) a criminal. This we found backed up the evidence collected by David Lammy in his review of the criminal justice system's treatment of non-white people.[55] It also suggested the problem was more fundamental than Lammy's analysis suggested, and this led to a discussion on why Lammy's recommendations would probably fail.

Whilst in the sections above I have focused predominately on the module's curriculum, I hope they have also illustrated the pedagogic approach used throughout its delivery. As Richard Hoggart has argued, "in a university, knowledge and teaching must be intertwined", and this was reflected in the role of my research in this module.[56] Also underpinning my approach was my strong belief that effective formative education is grounded in the way teachers behave with their students, how they make contact, how they listen and how they respond to students' contributions. My pedagogic practice seeks to create an engaging learning environment that extended well beyond the classroom and develops relationships of trust and respect. Drawing on Freire's concept of "problem-posing education" I sought to provide students with resources and opportunities to learn.[57] The module therefore included no formal lectures and was designed around a requirement to do either preparatory reading or watching, followed by workshops in which this preparatory material as well as additional material was discussed.[58] This proved challenging for the students who initially struggled to participate. However, as the module progressed, participation improved, and student confidence grew.

The module was assessed by a 3000-word essay (60%) and a 10-minute individual presentation (40%). Both had to be based on the same research and answer one of two questions:

(1) Critically evaluate the role of "race" in the criminal justice system of a British colony.
(2) Critically evaluate the concept of "crime" in the context of the history of the British empire.

Both questions required students to draw both on the history of colonialism and their disciplinary knowledge. Neither could be answered purely based on the content of an individual unit and students were required to undertake significant independent research. To support students, in addition to in-class (and in-train) support and office hours, each had an individual tutorial to review a draft and, following the marking of the coursework, a further individual tutorial to discuss developing their presentation. The quality of the work produced was generally good, with some students producing exceptional work. This reflected both student interest and the extensive level of research undertaken. All students submitted their coursework by the deadline and all, bar one who was ill, attended the presentations. All students passed the module.

---

[55]David Lammy, "The Lammy Review: An Independent Review into the Treatment of, and Outcomes for, Black, Asian and Minority Ethnic Individuals in the Criminal Justice System" (Ministry of Justice 2017) <https://assets.publishing.service.gov.uk/government/uploads/system/uploads/attachment_data/file/643001/lammy-review-final-report.pdf> accessed 29 October 2019.

[56]Richard Hoggart, *The Way We Live Now* (Chatto & Windus 1995) 23.

[57]Paulo Freire, *Pedagogy of the Oppressed* (Penguin Books 1996) 85.

[58]Although this pedagogy, and in particular the decision to not deliver lectures, was adopted for this module it recognises that it is not appropriate to all modules. On the wider debate concerning the appropriateness of the traditional lecture (see, for example, Sarah French and Gregor Kennedy, "Reassessing the Value of University Lectures" (2017) 22 Teaching in Higher Education 639) I remain agnostic.

Taking the module – student perspectives[59]

Five students were interviewed in late July/early August 2019 about their experiences of the module. The interviews were semi-structured and lasted between 12 and 40 minutes. The interviews started by focusing on students' motivations for taking the module. The module was seen as "something new" and "one of the most interesting", whilst one respondent said they chose it because, "by year three you know what you're interested in". Three specified a general interest in history, including one whose interest was clearly linked to the module's colonial focus, for her it was "kinda personal – getting fed up of the course – with racism – I wanted to know about the history. My parents are Jamaican." The remaining two students both also spoke about the importance of this focus; one "wanted to learn more about British Empire, about India" whilst the other "used to work with a guy from India and we had spoke about his history".

In terms of expectations, it was clear the students had not thought that deeply about the content in advance. One focused on the challenge, reporting they had "expect(ed) it to be hard, (involving a) lot more independent study", another, whilst having "no real expectations, wasn't expecting it to cover so many parts of the world". One student however had a clear expectation; they wanted: "More of an understanding, behind why it happened, what happened and why it wasn't criminalised, and we now don't take responsibility for what we did ... How and why it was acceptable at the time?"

All the respondents reported that they had not been familiar with the history covered in the module. Whilst they were "aware of some things" it was very superficial with another student commenting: "Stuff like the slave trade, you know it happened, you don't know how it happened, you don't know basic stuff of why it happened, how it started, how serious it got". Another "wasn't aware of the British empire in India", and felt the module had allowed her "to develop understanding of my family's history". For one student although "history at school was interesting", it was "never as far back as what we did". Two other students referred back to their studying of history at school. One reported that "we get taught stuff that happened in Germany, the Holocaust and stuff, don't really hear about this stuff" and another observed "when you study history – you don't get to focus on those countries". Across all the interviews it was clear that respondents recognised that their knowledge of colonial history had been partial and shallow, a position summed up by one student's observation that "talking to other members of the class, we were so oblivious to our own history".

All the respondents reported finding the module interesting with two claiming it was "fun". Three reported specifically that their developing interest in the topic resulting in high levels of engagement in independent research; "fully read around the topic", "went out to buy books", "I bought *Inglorious Empire*". One student identified the trip to Liverpool as the point when she really became "intrigued" by the subject matter. The

[59]As I had taught all the students interviewed, this research should be considered as insider research. Whilst my insider knowledge and my access to participants placed me in a unique position to undertake this research, it was also possible my position of power could distort students' answers (for a discussion on these issues see Carol Costley, Geoffrey C Elliott and Paul Gibbs, *Doing Work Based Research: Approaches to Enquiry for Insider-Researchers* (SAGE 2010)). To minimise these risks, all interviews took place after students had graduated (the one student who had outstanding work in another module was excluded). All the 12 students who had completed their studies were contacted, and seven students agreed to be interviewed. Two did not attend and limited time, and the quality of the data provided by the other five, meant they were not chased up and included in the research. Whilst I hope that my relationship with students would have allowed them to be entirely frank in their answers it is likely their responses were at least partly shaped by the fact that they were being interviewed by the lecturer who had designed and taught the module that they were being asked about.

breadth of topics covered was viewed positively, with one participant observing that "all (the) case studies (were) interesting and different, each topic was unique". One student highlighted "the link with crime theory" that ran through the module and how this was particularly interesting. Another felt that in her experience "lecturers hold back sometimes" but in this module she had been "surprised about how brutally honest it was". It had shown "how violent the past was and how dehumanised it was" and the student was "glad we got to look at it in such an honest way".

Students had mixed feelings about how the module was delivered, and particularly the absence of lectures. One student reported this approach was "at first very boring", but then "when we got into it, it was very interesting". They appreciated that it was "not just facts thrown at us" and observed that "you helped us understand it more by giving us documents and stuff to read". Like two other students she highlighted the impact that reading *Inglorious Empire* had had on her. Whilst another student asserted that "I personally prefer being taught things, rather than a discussion" she conceded by her third year she was not regularly attending classes, preferring to rely on lecturers' PowerPoint slides. Their absence on this module, she reported, "made me come in more". This style of learning meant that "our notes were unique". For her the key to the module's success was being "taught by someone who is also interested in the topic, ... you showed you cared as much as we should". All students acknowledged the difficulties they had experienced with the participatory nature of workshops and, whilst they in general understood what I was doing, conceded that "we didn't really talk much". As one student observed, "we are just used to copying the notes" before saying she was "grateful" for the approach, as without it she "wouldn't have had to read so much". Two students did not identify any benefit, with one highlighting the "lack of presentations" as a major weakness. Without PowerPoints, classes were "just looking through books", something that was "just too boring". The other student was convinced that there had been PowerPoint lectures throughout the module. In the interview I was unable to convince her that there were in fact none.

Overall, the students were positive about how the module was assessed. For one student, the "essay (was) quite hard, we had to get a lot in, really needed to read lots", whilst another appreciated there was no specified essay structure, which although this was "challenging", it was "nice to have that freedom". One student noted how the essay allowed students to "reflect back to other modules" and "think again about things". The choice of two questions was appreciated with one student who selected the "race" option observing that "if we only had the 'crime' option, I would have been less interested". The requirement to present based on the essay was seen as a "really good way of assessing us", with some reporting a preference for coursework over presentations and some an opposite preference, it was seen as "really fair". One student identified that "presentations allow you to learn from other students ... how they have understood things", identifying their role for cohort learning as well as assessment. Her experience had been that "sometimes a lecturer can present things, but it is difficult to understand, ... (whereas) when someone else simplifies it you get it". She suggested that consideration should be given to, after marking, sharing the coursework as well.

Only one student was unable to identify ways in which the module had been relevant to them personally. For the other four there was clear relevance. One reported "I didn't know much about India and Pakistan, my parents come from Pakistan" whilst another reported being able to participate when her "Dad & Uncle discussed Partition". Another reported talking about India to her (white British) grandmother, who "didn't even believe me, so I said, 'read this (a chapter from *Inglorious Empire*), it did happen'". Another student felt it had shown how the British empire "has shaped our country" whilst for another who described herself as white British, it had "opened my eyes" and that, unlike many (post)colonial subjects, she has been able to "keep my own name, keep my own language". For another student the module's content was:

> Very relevant ... we are still dealing with 'race' issues in the criminal justice system ... for me personally it really hit home, my brother gets stop and searched a few times when I was away at university ... it is close to home, it became really important for me ... 'race' isn't scientific ... this was really personal ...

All the students felt that, to some extent or other, the module had affected their wider understanding of the subject of criminology. One student reported that it had "helped me understand law" and that it was "so important to recognise actions that are not deemed criminal". Another observed that "criminology is about crime and in this module, we had to define crime", the module had made them "criticise things and analyse things more". A number reported that it had made them rethink their understanding of "crime" with one observing "enslaved Africans were property; it makes you think about property crime in a really different way". Students had clearly understood the module's link to criminological theory. One student observed that "some of the theories are quite old" and the module "provided the historical background to the time that people who wrote many of the criminological theories lived" allowing her "to interpret (these) theories in a different way".

Most of the students reported that they had not used the material from the module in their subsequent studies. This was unsurprising given how late in the programme it was delivered with, for example, one student reporting that "other modules (were) so different". One student did, however, report that in another assignment,

> I was discussing about being British and white, and how that can benefit me really, and I used some of the books to talk about white power, and how that, like being white benefited me, and how you can't change anything without acknowledging your own power in society.

Overall, the students felt positively about the module and the content. The main concern was the struggle they had experienced with participating. Whilst this was perceived to be largely a problem extending beyond this module, several suggestions were made. First, it was felt it was important not to "just dive in" on topics and supply more background information. One suggested that an online lecture, in advance of classes, that provided background information to the workshop topic would be helpful. Secondly, the provision of photocopied handouts of relevant chapters and other resources were regarded as a positive aspect of the module and two students asked if this could be extended. Thirdly, students felt a larger proportion of class time should be allocated to "teaching" with the workshop approach modified. Finally, students suggested that there should be more visits and they should occur earlier in the schedule. The overall critique of the module was positive with one student reporting it "was a great module" and another that it was "my favourite module, engaged in it, really enjoyed it".

Conclusion – a decolonised curriculum is more than a module

The module largely met its four key objectives. The history of the British empire proved to be an effective tool for critiquing key criminological concepts. Students recognised the weaknesses in criminologists' attempts to develop sociological definitions of "crime". In their coursework most students concluded that "crime" was essentially a legal construct which bore no direct relationship to notions of human rights or harm. Students' understandings of "race" and racism had, by the end of the module, changed in response to their exposure to colonial history. Whilst their understandings continued to be linked to their personal experiences, they were able to locate these in the context of structural racism. They also had new tools with which to explore how non-white people experience criminal justice in Britain today. By seeing state power being imposed on colonised society from the outside, students were able, in their coursework, to demonstrate a distinction between the state and the society it governs. The curriculum was perceived by all students as relevant. For white students, the colonial context made explicit the "whiteness" that generally lies hidden in the curriculum. For non-white students the module linked their studies to their family histories and provided intellectual tools to understand their own life experiences, both in general and in relation to the criminal justice system.

Whilst the module met its key objectives and introduced a (post/de)colonial perspective into the programme it should not be regarded as the successful decolonisation of a criminology degree. For the reasons set out above, criminology has a "colonial problem". The discipline's intimate relationship with the state, colonialism and racism means that further work is needed to establish whether criminology can be decolonised. If it can, a complete overhaul of the curriculum will be required. This will involve teaching the history of criminology (and its links to colonisation/racism), introducing non-western epistemologies relating to harm and conflict resolution, developing a theory of the state, exploring the colonial roots of the structural racism of criminal justice institutions, and recognising that "crime" is simply a legal construct. Most of all it will require acknowledging that "criminal man" and "criminal woman" are nothing more than a pseudo-scientific invention in the service of power.

Disclosure statement

No potential conflict of interest was reported by the author.

Creating the law school as a meeting place for epistemologies: decolonising the teaching of jurisprudence and human rights

Sophie Rigney

ABSTRACT

How do we create spaces within British law schools, for genuine engagement with decolonised methodologies and epistemologies? This paper examines an attempt to decolonise the curriculum in the rewriting of a module entitled "Justice, Law, and Human Rights", taught at the University of Dundee. I will reflect on the process of choosing the module topics and readings, and the successes and challenges of the course. I will consider the challenges of whether and how a non-Indigenous Australian can teach a decolonised law curriculum in Scotland. How does a teacher trained in Eurocentric and settler-colonial international law teach law, particularly in the colonial centre of the United Kingdom? How do we create space in a law school for Indigenous and non-Indigenous laws to meet?

How do we create spaces within British law schools, for genuine engagement with decolonised methodologies and epistemologies? How does a teacher trained in Eurocentric and settler-colonial international law teach, particularly when she is in the colonial centre of the United Kingdom (UK)? What should this teacher aspire to achieve in the classroom? This article addresses these questions through examining an attempt to decolonise the curriculum in a subject entitled "Justice, Law, and Human Rights", taught at the University of Dundee in Scotland. The article is structured in three parts. First, I outline some of the initial questions, concerns, and frameworks. Secondly, I examine how these have operated in the context of teaching "Justice, Law, and Human Rights". Finally, I reflect critically on this experience. In doing all this, I consider the challenges of whether and how a non-Indigenous Australian can teach and research a decolonised law curriculum in Scotland. I reflect on the challenges of attempting to create a space for student engagement with Indigenous legal epistemologies and ontologies.

In rewriting and attempting to decolonise this module, I have been aware of the question of how a white, non-Indigenous teacher like myself can teach on issues of decolonisation, race, and empire, without appropriating the space,[1] but while taking responsibility for the legal order in which I have been trained, and of which I am a

[1] Christine Schwöbel-Patel, "Decolonising the International Law Curriculum" <https://upload.sms.csx.cam.ac.uk/media/2914361> accessed 11 March 2019.

member. This is particularly true when a settler Australian teaches on the relationships of law between Indigenous nations, the settler-state, and the colonial power of the UK.[2] There is a significant literature amassing on the question of how settler teachers engage with decolonisation and the settler–Indigenous relationship.[3] However, much of this literature is focused on the experiences of teaching in settler-states (rather than in the UK). Moreover, the particular issue of how these questions play out in the context of legal education is not frequently analysed. This article attempts to think through some of these questions as they specifically relate to British law schools.

Part I: place/meeting

In this section, I will first offer details on my own location and where I come from; secondly, I will examine questions of place, meeting, and Indigenous legal epistemologies; and thirdly, I will examine three specific issues about what it means to attempt to create a British law school as a meeting place for Indigenous and non-Indigenous legal epistemologies, when I am a non-Indigenous, settler scholar.

It is important to set out my own place and how it relates to these questions.[4] I grew up in Hobart (nipaluna), Australia: the land of the muwinina people, one of the clans of the palawa, the Indigenous people of lutruwita (Tasmania).[5] The palawa people never ceded their sovereignty over this land, and it is likely that my ancestors were actively involved in their dispossession. By various constellations of circumstances, I lived in the UK for several years; and between 2017 and 2020, I lived in Scotland, working as a lecturer in law at the University of Dundee. As I finalise this article, I am living back in nipaluna, and working as a researcher at the Indigenous Law Centre at the University of New South Wales.

My "epistemic location"[6] is that I am trained in international law, and particularly, I have been trained and admitted to practice in the form of international law which "emerged alongside the modem European state system".[7] This form of international law is Eurocentric.[8] As an international lawyer trained in the territory now known as

---

[2]I use the term "Indigenous" to refer to First Nations Peoples. I would like to acknowledge, however, that many different peoples and nations are included in this term, and that this term is imperfect.

[3]See, for example, Lisa Korteweg and Tesa Fiddler, "Unlearning Colonial Identities While Engaging in Relationality: Settler Teachers' Education-as-Reconciliation" (2018) 53 McGill Journal of Education 254; Martin Cannon, "Changing the Subject in Teacher Education: Centering Indigenous, Diasporic, and Settler Colonial Relations" (2012) 4(2) Cultural and Pedagogical Inquiry 21; Jennifer Tupper, "The Possibilities for Reconciliation through Difficult Dialogues: Treaty Education as Peacebuilding" (2014) 44 Curriculum Inquiry 469; Jennifer Tupper and Michael Cappello, "Teaching Treaties as (Un)usual Narratives: Disrupting the Curricular Commonsense" (2018) 38 Curriculum Inquiry 559; Marc Higgins, Brooke Madden and Lisa Korteweg, "Witnessing (Halted) Deconstruction: White Teachers' 'Perfect Stranger' Position within Urban Indigenous Education" (2015) 18 Race, Ethnicity and Education 251; Fiona Nicoll, "'Are You Calling Me a Racist?': Teaching Critical Whiteness Theory in Indigenous Sovereignty" (2004) 3(2) Borderlands 112.

[4]I am particularly inspired by the use of vignettes and understanding of place in Mark McMillan, "Koowarta and the Rival Indigenous International: Our Place as Indigenous Peoples in the International" (2014) 23 Griffith Law Review 110; and the "location" work in Katie Boudreau Morris, "Decolonizing Solidarity: Cultivating Relationships of Discomfort" (2017) 7 Settler Colonial Studies 456.

[5]For more on the history of lutruwita/Tasmania and the palawa people, see Ida West, *Pride Against Prejudice: Reminiscences of a Tasmanian Aborigine* (Australian Institute of Aboriginal Studies 1984); Murray Johnson and Ian McFarlane, *Van Diemen's Land: An Aboriginal History* (UNSW Press 2015); Lyndall Ryan, *Tasmanian Aborigines: A History Since 1803* (Allen & Unwin 2012).

[6]Morris (n 4) 456.

[7]Anne Orford, "Ritual, Mediation and the International Laws of the South" (2007) 16 Griffith Law Review 353, 353.

[8]See eg Martti Koskenniemi, "Histories of International Law: Dealing with Eurocentrism" (2011) 19 Rechtsgeschitchte 152; Antony Anghie, *Imperialism, Sovereignty, and the Making of International Law* (CUP 2007).

Australia, the international law I was taught has an additional "gloss": it has advanced through a settler-colonial state.[9] The international law I have been admitted to practice, then, is European in origin but is also settler-colonial in application. This international law has been used to justify and support the settler-state, including through the application and maintenance of the doctrine of *terra nullius* and the continued non-justiciability of Indigenous sovereignties.[10] European international law and settler-colonialism are therefore concomitant.

In recent years, I have become more aware of the ways European international law has assisted colonisation[11] and more aware of the ways Indigenous peoples have practised a distinct form of international law for millennia. My approach to law and legal pedagogy has increasingly shifted to a place where I offer a critique of my discipline: that international legal scholarship has not adequately engaged with the ways Indigenous peoples undertake international law. To "live with honour according to law"[12] involves actively acknowledging the problems with the discipline of which I am a member, and to move towards meeting Indigenous international law as law.[13]

What do I mean, then, by "creating the law school as a meeting place for epistemologies"? There are three main elements to this: meeting, place, and epistemologies and ontologies. First, let us start with the physical location and what it means – the "place" of the law school. The ideas of "space" and "place" – and the differences and relationships between them – have "long histories", multiple meanings and "connotations which reverberate with other debates and many aspects of life".[14] These are highly theorised concepts, particularly in the fields of decolonial geography, critical legal geography, and critical pedagogy of place.[15] For present purposes, I found Ross Gibson to offer a useful definition of space and place: place is

> the shared, custodial scene in which we offer, debate, narrate, subvert or maintain meanings that can orient and guide us in the turbulent world of fate, nature and power. Place is a custodial

---

[9]For more on settler colonialism, see Corey Snelgrove, Rita Kaur Dhamoon and Jeff Corntassel, "Unsettling Settler Colonialism: The Discourse and Politics of Settlers, and Solidarity with Indigenous Nations" (2014) 3(2) Decolonization: Indigeneity, Education & Society 1.

[10]See Dianne Otto, "A Question of Law or Politics? Indigenous Claims to Sovereignty in Australia" (1995) 21 Syracuse Journal of International Law and Commerce 65, 66; Phillip Falk and Gary Martin, "Misconstruing Indigenous Sovereignty: Maintaining the Fabric of Australian Law" in Aileen Moreton-Robinson (ed), *Sovereign Subjects: Indigenous Sovereignty Matters* (Allen & Unwin 2007) 33, 34.

[11]See particularly Anghie (n 8); S James Anaya, *Indigenous Peoples in International Law* (OUP 2000); Robert A Williams, *Savage Anxieties: The Invention of Western Civilization* (Palgrave Macmillan Trade 2012); Irene Watson, *Aboriginal Peoples, Colonialism and International Law: Raw Law* (Routledge 2014).

[12]On non-Indigenous lawyers acting with "honour", see Shaun McVeigh, "Law as (More or Less) Itself: On Some Not Very Reflective Elements of Law" (2014) 4 UC Irvine Law Review 471; Orford (n 7), 353; Sundhya Pahuja, "Laws of Encounter: A Jurisdictional Account of International Law" (2013) 1 London Review of International Law 63.

[13]For more on Indigenous International Law, see Sophie Rigney, "Towards Meeting Indigenous International Law" (draft, on file with author); see also Amar Bhatia, "The South of the North: Building on Critical Approaches to International Law with Lessons from the Fourth World" (2012) 14 Oregon Review of International Law 131.

[14]Doreen Massey, *Space, Place, and Gender* (University of Minnesota Press 1994) 1.

[15]See particularly Eve Tuck and Marcia McKenzie, *Place in Research: Theory, Methodology, and Methods*(Routledge 2015); Nicholas Blomley and Joel Bakan, "Spacing Out: Towards a Critical Geography of Law" (1992) 30 Osgoode Hall Law Journal 661; Sarah de Leeuw and Sarah Hunt, "Unsettling Decolonising Geographies" (2018) 12(7) Geography Compass 1; David Gruenewald, "The Best of Both Worlds: A Critical Pedagogy of Place" (2003) 32(4) Educational Researcher 3; Robert Stevenson, "A Critical Pedagogy of Place and the Critical Place(s) of Pedagogy" (2008) 14 Environmental Education Research 353; Kate McCoy, Eve Tuck and Marcia McKenzie (eds), *Land Education: Rethinking Pedagogies of Place from Indigenous, Postcolonial and Decolonizing Perspectives* (Routledge 2016).

> phenomenon [...] while space is a neutral entity awaiting significance or value. Space can become "territory" or "property" if appropriated in particular ways. Or it can become "place" if incorporated more assiduously and ritually into systems that give rise to personal and/or communal awareness.[16]

Another useful way of thinking about "space" has been offered by Doreen Massey, who argues that space is constituted by interrelations, that it is a sphere in which multiple trajectories exist, and that it is always under construction.[17] This understanding of space is useful when thinking about how different legal systems can meet. But keeping in mind Gibson's warning that "space" can be appropriated into "property" or "territory" if we are not careful, how can we ensure that the site of the law school moves from "space" to "place"? We must attend to "personal and/or communal awareness", and "custodianship", specifically about law. As will become more apparent in the remainder of this article, creating the law school as a meeting place for epistemologies will be about two main strands, both of which involve personal and communal awareness about law, and custodianship of law: first, being responsible for the law that we are trained in; and second, acknowledging other modes of knowing and doing law.

Let me make clear that a role of "being responsible for the law we are trained in" does not mean taking an uncritical position in relation to that law. Rather, it suggests that we must know what the law is; understand that as people trained in it, we are partly responsible for how it manifests or changes; and acknowledge the various harms enabled or caused by that law, as well as its structural conditions and what it makes possible. Being responsible for one's law can be both an acknowledgement and a refusal: an acknowledgement of what has been done in the name of that law, and, perhaps, a refusal to accept this as appropriate. As Seow Hon Tan has noted (regarding teaching jurisprudence and legal virtue), "to be effective guardians (of their legal system), students need a keen understanding of what is worthy of preservation".[18] Being responsible for one's law is also linked to acknowledging other legal epistemologies and ontologies, because being responsible for the law one is trained in involves also being responsible for how it relates to other laws. These ideas will be given more detail below.

Next, let us turn to "meeting", and "epistemologies and ontologies". The law school can be a site for bolstering law's hegemony and its violence.[19] For example, as mentioned above, international law has been used to claim that Indigenous sovereignties are non-justiciable, and has been used to strengthen the settler-state – but this side of international law is not often taught in law schools, or critically engaged with in popularly assigned textbooks. In this way, the law school may deny these aspects of international law, and in doing so, can enhance the position and power of international law. Alternatively, though, the law school can be a powerful site for bringing different legal systems into relation or into conversation. It can be, as in Gibson's definition, a space

---

[16]Ross Gibson, "Skerrick Scenes" in Gus Worby and Lester-Irabinna Rigney (eds), *Sharing Spaces: Indigenous and Non-Indigenous Responses to Story, Country and Rights* (API Network 2006) 8, 8.

[17]Massey (n 14).

[18]Seow Hon Tan, "Teaching Legal Ideals through Jurisprudence" (2009) 43 The Law Teacher 14, 26.

[19]See, for example, Duncan Kennedy, "Legal Education and the Reproduction of Hierarchy" (1982) 32 Journal of Legal Education 591. For more on the violence of law, see Austin Sarat (ed), *Law, Violence, and the Possibility of Justice* (Princeton University Press 2001); Nicholas Blomley, "Law, Property, and the Geography of Violence: The Frontier, the Survey, and the Grid" (2003) 93 Annals of the Association of American Geographers 121; Julie Evans, "Where Lawlessness Is Law: The Settler-Colonial Frontier as a Legal Space of Violence" (2009) 30 Australian Feminist Law Journal 3.

where we can "offer, debate, narrate, subvert or maintain meanings that can orient and guide us in the turbulent world of fate, nature and power". In this way, the law school can be a meeting place for different "meanings" – two (or more) legal systems and their attendant ways of knowing and doing law – and can be a place where they are brought into a relationship. In considering the law school as a meeting place of laws, I am drawing particularly on the work of Shaunnagh Dorsett and Shaun McVeigh, who write that common law jurisprudence:

> continues to struggle to create an appropriate form and conduct of the relations between itself and Indigenous laws and jurisprudence. It has struggled, in short, to create an appropriate meeting place of laws.[20]

However, before this conversation – or meeting of laws – can be done, the different legal systems and their epistemologies must be acknowledged and afforded respect.

Indigenous communities create law, exercise sovereignty, practise jurisdiction over territory, and possess political structures. This has occurred for millennia, and continues to this day.[21] Indigenous conceptions of sovereignty are in a relationship with the land as a source of life, law, culture, and spirituality.[22] Such sovereignties are location-specific and tied to jurisdiction: Indigenous nations exercise jurisdiction and sovereignty within their mutually recognised national boundaries.[23] Ways of practising law and governance, and enacting sovereignty are diverse: "Each Indigenous nation has different laws, institutions and practices, derived from its experiences, beliefs and country".[24] The invasion of Australia by the British and the processes of colonisation were devastating to Indigenous systems of law, but Indigenous legal systems have persisted.[25]

This existence of Indigenous legal epistemologies and ontologies has often been denied. Most profoundly, in the Australian context, was the invocation of the doctrine of *terra nullius* or "land belonging to no one", which was eventually used to justify the British claim to the territory. This was a denial, both of people, and of their systems of governance and law. The denial of Indigenous law as law is inherently colonial, and is a form of violence.[26] Yet this denial continues in law schools around the world when we do not acknowledge Indigenous law and do not place Indigenous law in conversation with other laws.

Instead of perpetuating this denial, we can instead work towards engaging in a relationship between legal orders. Acknowledging Indigenous law means that we can start a conversation between multiple legal jurisdictions. Mark McMillan has written that "In order to understand a jurisdictional boundary or meeting point there must be a

---

[20]Shaunnagh Dorsett and Shaun McVeigh, "Conduct of Laws: Native Title, Responsibility, and Some Limits of Jurisdictional Thinking" (2012) 36 Melbourne University Law Review 470.

[21]Recent excavations prove Indigenous peoples have lived with Australian land for at least 65,000 years and some of the artefacts may be up to 80,000 years old <www.theguardian.com/australia-news/2017/jul/19/dig-finds-evidence-of-aboriginal-habitation-up-to-80000-years-ago> accessed 27 October 2020. Indigenous peoples understand that they have lived with the land since creation.

[22]Christine Black, *The Land Is the Source of the Law: A Dialogic Encounter with Indigenous Jurisprudence* (Routledge 2010).

[23]For more on Indigenous nationhood in the Australian context, see Stephen Cornell, "Processes of Native Nationhood: The Indigenous Politics of Self-Government" (2015) 6(4) The International Indigenous Policy Journal, Article 4.

[24]Anna Dziedzic and Mark McMillan, "Australian Indigenous Constitutions: Recognition and Renewal" (2016) 44 Federal Law Review 337, 342–43.

[25]ibid.

[26]See Sophie Rigney, "Indigenous Nationhood, Political Relationships, and Transitional Justice: Addressing Australia's Political Violence" (draft, on file with author).

recognition of the structured existences of the other to observe (and respect) its jurisdiction".[27] In order to create the law school as a meeting place for different legal epistemologies, we must first acknowledge those laws.

Further, if we think with jurisdiction, as Sundhya Pahuja notes, there are two implications. First, we are able to hear "the indigenous law as law, which other forms of engagement do not"; and secondly, we are in a position where "we must choose our law, rather than assuming any one law is simply already there before we arrive, as the law which simply 'governs', in some detached and transcendent way".[28] Rather than seeing "law" as a universal, we must see the law that we are trained in as just one mode of law, which can exist in conversation or meeting with other laws.

If the denial of Indigenous law is inherently colonial, it is also true that acknowledging Indigenous legal epistemologies – and genuinely engaging with them – is part of a decolonial practice. Decolonisation, in Foluke Adebisi's words, "asks for critical inclusion of epistemologies, ways of knowing, lived experiences, texts and scholarly work that have been previously excluded from our disciplines".[29] Linda Tuhiwai Smith has outlined particular "projects" that Indigenous people undertake to "decolonise methodologies" in order to "reclaim, reformulate and reconstitute" Indigenous cultures and languages.[30] Of particular importance for this article are the projects of claiming, whereby Indigenous peoples make "claims and assertions" about their "rights and dues", and are a way of teaching "both the non-indigenous audience and the new generations of indigenous peoples an official account of their collective story"; story-telling, where there is a "focus on dialogue and conversations amongst ourselves as indigenous peoples, to ourselves and for ourselves. Such approaches fit well with the oral traditions which are still a reality in day-to-day indigenous lives"; and writing, whereby Indigenous authors write work that will be read by both Indigenous and non-Indigenous audiences.[31]

But what does it mean for a non-Indigenous, settler scholar to do this? And what does it mean to do this in the UK? The inclusion of Indigenous legal epistemologies is complicated here for several reasons. First, because I am not Indigenous, I cannot myself know fully what Indigenous law is. Indigenous legal epistemologies are "layered", with some layers accessible to the public while others are exclusively for "those who know", such as elders and custodians of law.[32] My understanding of Indigenous law, as someone who is not Indigenous, is necessarily incomplete. This is a challenge, particularly as a teacher: classrooms are often predicated on the belief that a teacher will hold knowledge, which they will then transmit to students. Without holding this knowledge, I cannot be an authority on this issue. This lack of authority can be particularly challenging for a teacher who is both female, and early in her career (as I am). Tertiary teachers are often held to different standards depending on their gender, race, and perceived status as an expert. As a white person, I have a particular privilege in the classroom,[33] even though I simultaneously lack authority

[27] McMillan (n 4) 118.

[28] Pahuja (n 12) 92.

[29] Foluke Adebisi, "Speaking of Decolonization, Law, Race and the Legal Curriculum at SLSA 2018" <http://slsablog.co.uk/blog/blog-posts/speaking-of-decolonization-law-race-and-the-legal-curriculum-at-slsa-2018/> accessed 11 March 2019.

[30] Linda Tuhiwai Smith, *Decolonise methodologies: Research and Indigenous Peoples* (Zed Books 1999).

[31] ibid 142–61.

[32] Watson (n 11) 43.

[33] Research shows that "instructors who are female and persons of color receive lower scores on ordinal student evaluations than those who are white males": Kerry Chávez and Kristina MW Mitchell, "Exploring Bias in Student Evaluations: Gender, Race, and Ethnicity" (2020) 53 Political Science and Politics 270.

on this issue. As a younger and female teacher, my lack of authority may be more noticeable or problematic for students. However, I do not subscribe to the idea that, as a teacher, I should be viewed as a special holder of knowledge, and indeed, I believe it is crucial to acknowledge the limits of my knowledge.[34] Further, I consider this to be an important opportunity to practise being in discomfort and humble in a state of unknowing. Settler scholars do not need to know everything all the time. A demand to know is itself imperial, and must be rejected by a settler teacher.

Secondly, there is a particular challenge for teaching on Indigenous legal epistemologies and ontologies in the UK: here, there is a denial of responsibility for their role in settler-colonies. Mark McMillan and I have written that the relationship between the Australian state and the colonial power of Great Britain allows both of these entities to deny their responsibility for harms committed against Indigenous people.[35] There is a mutual denial: "the emergence of the Australian state independent from the colonial power", we have written, "has obscured which entity must be held accountable for past harms to Indigenous populations ... the state of Australia can deny their past responsibility, and at the same moment, Great Britain can deny any ongoing responsibility".[36] This denial of responsibility in the UK – and a sense that the question of Indigenous Australians is something that occurs "over there" rather than "here" – is, I suggest, reflected in British law schools. Other questions linked to Britain's colonial past may have clearer links to British responsibility, but there is a sense that Indigenous peoples in settler-colonies are (in this case) the responsibility of Australia rather than the UK. The need to challenge this distance, and sense of being unaffected by the issue, was why I felt it important to address Indigenous people's rights in a course that was examining British human rights issues. I also felt that there was an opportunity – in teaching students living in Scotland[37] – to teach students who understood, or were regularly being exposed to, a history of place where people were both colonised and coloniser. Students may have had knowledge of the Highland Clearances and crofting;[38] of English invasions into Scotland; and of complicated understandings of sovereignty, due to Scottish devolution. They may have also had some knowledge of Scotland's role in slavery or colonial administrations. This complex history of Scottish colonisation and colonising opened a particular possibility to discuss British responsibility in settler-colonies.

Thirdly, I want to pause on what it means to be not just non-Indigenous, but a settler. I want to draw here on Katie Boudreau Morris's understandings of "decolonising solidarity".[39] In turn, she has drawn on the work of Harsha Walia who has called for replacing "a politics of solidarity" with Indigenous peoples, with "a practice of decolonisation".[40] This involves non-Indigenous people being "active and integral participants in a decolonisation movement". Decolonisation is "as much a process as a goal" and "it requires a profound recentering on Indigenous worldviews ... decolonisation is a

[34] I have been inspired by the writings of bell hooks, particularly *Teaching to Transgress: Education as the Practice of Freedom* (Routledge 1994) and *Teaching Critical Thinking: Practical Wisdom* (Routledge 2009).

[35] Mark McMillan and Sophie Rigney, "Race, Reconciliation and Justice in Australia: From Denial to Acknowledgment" (2018) 41 Race and Ethnic Studies 759.

[36] ibid 764.

[37] Some of the students were Scottish, but many were from Northern Ireland, England, and parts of the world that accept an English qualifying law degree.

[38] See eg TM Devine, *The Scottish Clearances: A History of the Dispossessed, 1600-1900* (Penguin 2019).

[39] Morris (n 4).

[40] ibid 458.

dramatic reimagining of relationships with land, people, and the state. Much of this requires study. It requires conversation. It is a practice; it is an unlearning."[41] Eve Tuck and K Wayne Yang have pointed out that "decolonisation" can often be invoked as a metaphor, and that there are several ways in which settlers move to bolster their own innocence.[42] Instead, they say, decolonisation is unsettling, and should be unsettling.[43] These points of centring Indigenous worldviews, reimagining relationships with land, people and the state, and unlearning and being unsettled, are all aspects which I draw on in this article and which I am still in a process of working with.

Part II: teaching "Justice, Law, and Human Rights"

"Justice, Law, and Human Rights" is an Honours module that is offered to all law students in their penultimate or ultimate year of study at the University of Dundee. Depending on their degree structure, for some students the module was compulsory, and for some it was optional. The module aims to provide "an in-depth examination of topical human rights issues in the UK".[44] It links jurisprudence with human rights law.

In 2019, I taught the module for the first time, together with a then-colleague. On inheriting the module, we decided to completely rewrite it; however, we had some constraints: the module had to address human rights issues, it had to be based in the UK, and it had to deal with jurisprudence. I decided to teach my seminars on the issues of slavery and contemporary reparations and responsibility for historical slavery; Indigenous peoples and justice; the rights of citizenship and the "Windrush generation"; and war crimes allegedly committed by British forces, particularly in Iraq. Each of these issues had in common the question of how the British state relates to its citizens or people it has a responsibility to; and also the question of whether and how the British state is responsible for its actions around the world. A benefit of the focus on the UK was that the module could be reasonably place-based. For example, in the class on slavery, we examined the University of Glasgow's reparations for slavery. I also raised Dundee's role in the slave trade – particularly through the trade in jute, manufactured in Dundee – and invited students to discuss whether the University of Dundee should investigate its role in this history and whether reparations are needed.

I was of the opinion that the module aim, "to look at rights in the UK through different jurisprudential lenses", lent itself to opening up what is considered to be "jurisprudence" beyond the "traditional canon" of law. This is particularly so because jurisprudence is a useful site to examine morality and values, and law's relation to them.[45] In this way, teaching jurisprudence can move students from "accepting and learning the law as it stands and limiting the power of their critique to piecemeal reform, to questioning foundational assumptions".[46] Teaching a diversity of approaches to legal theory can further heighten these benefits of jurisprudence. I therefore inserted into the module "critical approaches to law", which I linked to the seminars on slavery

[41] ibid.
[42] Eve Tuck and K Wayne Yang, "Decolonization Is Not a Metaphor" (2012) 1 Decolonization: Indigeneity, Education & Society 1, 9.
[43] ibid 3.
[44] University of Dundee, Justice, Law and Human Rights Module Guide, 2018/19.
[45] See Tan (n 18).
[46] ibid 19.

and to Indigenous peoples; "critical race theory", which I used to address the issue of citizenship and the "Windrush generation"; and "feminist legal theories", which I taught in the class on war and war crimes.

In picking the readings and the remit of each seminar, I was guided by the requirements of the module, and an aim that each seminar would address a particular form of jurisprudential thought, and also a particular human rights mechanism. For the seminar on Indigenous peoples, I decided to focus on the repatriation of Indigenous objects and remains from British museums. This linked the responsibility of the UK in the present day to questions of Indigenous rights.

Ultimately, the seminar addressed Indigenous Australians and their relationships with the settler-state and the colonial power of the UK, in three particular respects:

(1) How useful human rights, and critical legal studies, are for Indigenous justice claims;
(2) Repatriation of remains and objects as a particular justice claim;
(3) The conduct of lawful relations and the relationships between coloniser, settler, and Indigenous peoples.

I want to pause on the first of these. This was a human rights course, but I was clear in this seminar that Indigenous rights are not just a human rights issue. This is because while human rights language and law are frequently used to frame Indigenous justice claims and Indigenous–colonial relationships, this can obfuscate both the power and sovereignty of Indigenous groups and also the colonial cause of rights issues. This is a question of how two sovereign entities relate on stolen land; and decolonisation demands more than what human rights frameworks can usefully provide.[47] So in teaching "Justice, Law, and Human Rights", I explicitly raised the limitations of human rights language and law for Indigenous justice claims, and that thinking of these issues in terms of Indigenous sovereignty and law can be powerful. In class, we discussed Indigenous nationhood, governance, and legal systems; and Indigenous law was placed as the starting point for our discussions and learning.

The three aspects of Indigenous justice examined in class determined the choice of required readings, which were:

- Robert A Williams, "Taking Rights Aggressively: The Perils and Promise of Critical Legal Theory for Peoples of Colour" (1987) 5 Law & Inequality: A Journal of Theory and Practice 103
- Shaun McVeigh, "Jurisprudent of London: Arts of Association" (2016) 20 Law Text Culture 189
- Paul Daley, "Preservation or Plunder? The Battle over the British Museum's Indigenous Australian Show" *The Guardian* (London, 9 April 2015)
- United Nations Declaration on the Rights of Indigenous Peoples
- British Museum Act 1963, s.3(4)
- Sarah Keenan, "The Gweagal Shield" (2017) 68 Northern Ireland Legal Quarterly 283

I picked the first of these because Robert Williams does two things that were particularly relevant. First, he discusses "whether critical legal theory can be of assistance" to

[47] See Tuck and Yang (n 42), particularly at 3.

Indigenous justice projects.[48] In particular, he critiques the critical legal studies (CLS) movement and the "contempt, hostility, and suspicion of 'rights' discourse" that the CLS movement and authors have generated.[49] I used this as a counter-argument to some of the critical legal theory I had discussed with students earlier in the module. Secondly, Williams lays bare Eurocentric readings of events. The article commences with a "parable" about an "Indian Grandfather" and an elevator, before "revealing" an alternative possibility: that the "Grandfather" was actually playing on the prejudices of the white people, who underestimate him.[50] This clear articulation of Eurocentric and prejudicial approaches was useful at the start of a class on Indigenous justice claims.

I want to focus on one of these readings in particular: Shaun McVeigh's "Jurisprudent of London". McVeigh addresses the "two linked exhibitions by the British Museum and the Australian National Museum", framing them as a jurisprudential encounter. He argues that these exhibitions were "both concerned with the insistence on, and invitation to, the conduct of lawful relations. In response, the question is 'What might it mean for a jurisprudent of London to respond well to such an invitation and insistence?'"[51]

I chose this article partly for its dealing with the issue of repatriation of Indigenous objects and remains, but also because of McVeigh's articulation of the importance that "those who live by the common law tradition are responsible for the care of their own law and the conduct of their lawful relations".[52] The obligations of these jurists may even be reasonably simple: "know your law, acknowledge the relationship of laws, and respond with the appropriate protocols".[53] McVeigh works with the research of Indigenous jurisprudents to consider the relationship between Indigenous and non-Indigenous laws. This article builds on McVeigh's significant work (often together with Dorsett) on the "conduct of lawful relations".[54]

I chose this article because I wanted students to think about their law. What does it mean to be a Scottish, English, Northern Irish jurist? What does it mean to be a lawyer trained in these laws – which have been fundamental to colonisation, and remain crucial to the continued possession by the British Museum of Indigenous objects? Further, what does it mean to engage in a lawful relationship with Indigenous peoples and legal systems? We asked those questions in class and reflected on them.

Part III: critical reflections

In hindsight, I am aware that I did not do enough to decolonise the module, and there are several things I would do differently if I taught a similar module in future. There are five things to focus on: outlining different approaches to law; more discussion on "choosing law"; more Indigenous authors and dialogues between Indigenous and non-Indigenous authors; greater attention to the global links of empire and also the local place of learning; and more discussion on land rights and settler complicity.

---

[48] Robert A Williams, "Taking Rights Aggressively: The Perils and Promise of Critical Legal Theory for Peoples of Colour" (1987) 5 Law & Inequality: A Journal of Theory and Practice 103, 104.
[49] ibid.
[50] ibid, particularly at 104–11.
[51] Shaun McVeigh, "Jurisprudent of London: Arts of Association" (2016) 20 Law Text Culture 189, 190.
[52] ibid.
[53] McVeigh (n 51) 191.
[54] Shaunnagh Dorsett and Shaun McVeigh, *Jurisdiction* (Routledge 2012); see also Dorsett and McVeigh (n 20).

Taking these in turn, first, I would build in more time to discuss different critical approaches to law. I would do this as an introductory seminar. In 2019, I addressed these different jurisprudential approaches (critical legal studies, critical race theory, and so on) seminar by seminar, linked to the issue we were discussing. However, a class dedicated to these theories initially would better equip students to understand law as violence, as contested, and that it may be otherwise. Morris has pointed out that there is often a genuine good intention on the part of non-Indigenous people, "but a dearth of tools and accurate personal knowledge for engaging those intentions".[55] Part of the role of the teacher, then, is to provide students with the tools to engage their intentions towards decoloniality. Students told me that they had never before come across critical approaches to law, and instead had been taught in a very doctrinal way.[56] Spending more time analysing approaches to law which demonstrate law's relationships to race and empire – and having this as a framework – would better provide students with tools to further their decolonial activism.[57]

Secondly, I would encourage greater reflection on choosing law and jurisprudence. We did deal with this in class, through the McVeigh article, but some more dedicated time early in the semester would have been beneficial. A greater introduction for students on their roles, responsibilities and powers as lawyers – and in particular, common law or Scots lawyers – would have been useful for this seminar, and for other seminars on issues like reparations for slavery. These are complex questions, and framing the course on these issues rather than raising them during the class on Indigenous justice claims would have been a clearer way to work with the students to address these ideas.

Thirdly, I failed in setting sufficient Indigenous scholarship into the required reading. There is only one Indigenous author on the list of required reading.[58] The list of "recommended reading" for the module had a greater proportion of Indigenous writers.[59] If the aim was to create a relationship between Indigenous and non-Indigenous jurisprudences, there needs to be more Indigenous jurisprudence on the reading list. Because I am not Indigenous, and my knowledge can only ever be partial, it is important that the reading list reflects and centres the knowledges of Indigenous scholars who can write on their own legal epistemologies.

I would like to take this further, and create a dialogue between Indigenous and non-Indigenous authors, via the site of the reading list and then the classroom. I would do this by pairing different articles together so that they operate in conversation. Such an

---

55 Morris (n 4) 459.

56 This does not necessarily mean that other teachers were not using critical approaches to law. It is possible that they were doing so but were not explicitly discussing this with the students.

57 The first reading for students was Susan Marks, "Human Rights in Disastrous Times" in James Crawford and Martti Koskenniemi (eds), *The Cambridge Companion to International Law* (CUP 2012). I used this to draw attention to ideas of law and human rights as being not neutral but rather political. This was probably the closest to a "framework" for introducing critical approaches to law.

58 Although the United Nations Declaration on the Rights of Indigenous Peoples could also be viewed as "Indigenous authored".

59 The list: Robert A Williams Jr, "Encounters on the Frontiers of International Human Rights Law: Redefining the Terms of Indigenous Peoples' Survival in the World" (1990) 39 Duke Law Journal 660; Costas Douzinas and Adam Gearey, *Critical Jurisprudence: The Political Philosophy of Justice* (Bloomsbury 2005) 283–92; Mark McMillan and Sophie Rigney, "The Place of the First Peoples in the International Sphere: A Logical Starting Point for the Demand for Justice by Indigenous Peoples" (2016) 39 Melbourne University Law Review 981; Aileen Moreton-Robinson, *The White Possessive: Property, Power, and Indigenous Sovereignty* (University of Minnesota Press 2015); Gaye Sculthorpe, *The BP Exhibition Indigenous Australia: Enduring Civilisation* (British Museum Press 2015).

approach would have several benefits. First, it would hopefully give greater meaning and structure for students as they think through "the conduct of lawful relations" and the idea of "choosing one's law" and their own responsibilities as legal practitioners. Secondly, it would advance the idea of creating the law school as a genuine meeting place for various legal epistemologies and ontologies, and facilitating a conversation between those ways of knowing and doing law. Conversation is a well-established Indigenous methodology,[60] and Indigenous authors have paired with non-Indigenous authors on many occasions, to write articles as a practice of conversation. An example is an article I wrote with Mark McMillan, a Wiradjuri (Indigenous) academic. We wrote that:

> we come to this article from different backgrounds, and seek to bring different approaches to the question [...] We do this from the positions of Indigenous and non-Indigenous. This conversation, an act of storytelling, is in furtherance of exerting and practising our distinct jurisprudences – to each other, the international, the domestic and the Indigenous international.[61]

In that article, Mark and I were "engaged in a dialogue that rests upon [our] different approaches to, and experiences of, international law"; and that conversation (of writing together) was occurring "in order to better understand our respective ways of knowing".[62]

I would also involve students in creating the seminar list, the reading list, the sets of reflections for class, and the assessment tasks, so that they co-create the curriculum.[63] Students have been active in the decolonising the curriculum movement,[64] and I am confident that Dundee's students would have made important contributions to a decolonised curriculum.[65] Inviting the students to co-create the curriculum would also align with my values to create a classroom where the teacher is not assumed to be a special holder of knowledge. I did not do this in 2019 largely due to limitations on my labour: I had a phased return to work after parental leave; I returned to work not long before teaching recommenced; and my workload was significantly overloaded. I simply did not have time to be as reflective as I would have liked, or to engage students in this way. I hope that, in future, I will have greater ability to engage in genuine co-creation of the curriculum with the students.

Fourthly, I would make more explicit the links between settler-colonialism and "imperialism all around the globe"[66] and how Indigenous issues in Australia are linked to the other issues in the course, particularly slavery, and the Windrush scandal. I addressed the seminars as largely separate, with some cross-reference to questions of empire and race. However, I would restructure this to connect the decolonial struggles around the world more clearly. As Tuck and Yang write,

---

60 See Margaret Kovach, "Conversational Method in Indigenous Research" (2010) 5(1) First Peoples Child and Family Review 40; Snelgrove, Dhamoon and Corntassel (n 9); Worby and Rigney (n 16); McMillan and Rigney (n 59).

61 McMillan and Rigney (n 59) 984.

62 ibid.

63 See Catherine Bovill and Cherie Woolmer, "How Conceptualisations of Curriculum in Higher Education Influence Staff-Student Creation *in* and *of* the Curriculum" (2019) 78 Higher Education 407; Catherine Bovill and others, "Addressing Potential Challenges in Co-creating Learning and Teaching: Overcoming Resistance, Navigating Institutional Norms and Ensuring Inclusivity in Student-Staff Partnerships" (2016) 71 Higher Education 195.

64 See, for example, the student-led "Decolonising the Curriculum" project at Kent Law School, and the student involvement in "Decolonising SOAS".

65 An example of a decolonised and co-created curriculum is explored in Jess Crilly, Lucy Panesar and Zey Suka-Bill, "Co-constructing a Liberated/Decolonised Arts Curriculum" (2020) 17(2) Journal of University Teaching & Learning Practice Article 9.

66 Tuck and Yang (n 42) 31.

> Decolonization "here" is intimately connected to anti-imperialism elsewhere. However, decolonial struggles here/there are not parallel, not shared equally, nor do they bring neat closure to the concerns of all involved – particularly not for settlers. Decolonization is not equivocal to other anti-colonial struggles. It is incommensurable.[67]

I would also be more explicit with the history of race and empire in Scotland and specifically in Dundee. I did this in the seminar on slavery, but in line with critical pedagogy of place, it would have been useful to connect the place of learning to multiple topics. The emphasis of the module on "the UK" rather than on "Scotland" or even "Dundee" could have obfuscated the very real links between Dundee, imperialism, and human rights issues worldwide.

And fifth, I would place more emphasis on land rights and more on settler benefits and complicity. Decolonisation is, at its core, about land.[68] In a conversation with one student, I acknowledged that I had personally benefited from capital which had been passed down through generations of my family – capital which was based on land that had been stolen – and that I have not done enough to remedy that and to engage in proper distribution of my wealth. It goes deeper than this, though – it is also about challenging my relationship with the land, which is a relationship that has been based on possession and productivity,[69] and as we come to a point in the climate crisis where this is increasingly unsustainable, it is incumbent on us to decolonise our own relationships with land and to encourage students to think about this more deeply.[70]

Some tentative conclusions

Decolonisation is a process, and because it is rightly radical, it is also discomforting and must challenge current assumptions, denials, and power imbalances. Tuck and Yang point out that decolonisation should be material, not metaphor: it involves "interruptions which destabilise, unbalance, and repatriate the very terms and assumptions of some of the most radical efforts to reimagine human power relations".[71] Morris notes that, in decolonising solidarity, there is an "importance of listening to our discomforts, sitting with them and wading through them, and then deploying them towards decolonization. And then listening to them again and again."[72] In the classroom, discomfort is a challenging emotion and a challenging pedagogical environment. This is one reason why teaching in a decolonial way is so difficult. However, while the discomfort (and anger, fear, shame, and guilt) that may be felt by students and settler scholars is challenging, it can also be productive.[73] If listened to carefully, and then

---

[67]ibid.

[68]Morris (n 4) 469; Tuck and Yang (n 42), particularly at 5. This is not to say that decolonisation is *only* about land, but in the settler-colonial context, issues of Indigenous land rights and the benefits gained by settlers from appropriating Indigenous lands are fundamental.

[69]Drawing particularly on Tuck and Yang (n 42), particularly at 6; Moreton-Robinson (n 59).

[70]On Indigenous approaches to the climate crisis, see Philip Marrii Winzer, "We Need a Blak New Deal to Fight the Climate Crisis" *Overland* (19 September 2019) https://overland.org.au/2019/09/we-need-a-blak-new-deal-to-fight-the-climate-crisis/ last accessed 27 October 2020; Tony Birch, "Climate Change, Recognition and Social Place-Making" *Sydney Review of Books* (3 March 2017) <https://sydneyreviewofbooks.com/climate-change-recognition-and-caring-for-country/>accessed 24 September 2019; Teila Watson, "Indigenous Knowledge Systems Can Help Solve the Problems of Climate Change" *The Guardian* (London, 2 June 2017) <www.theguardian.com/commentisfree/2017/jun/02/indigenous-knowledge-systems-can-help-solve-the-problems-of-climate-change> accessed 24 September 2019.

[71]Tuck and Yang (n 42) 28.

[72]Morris (n 4) 457.

[73]Megan Boler, *Feeling Power: Emotions and Education* (Routledge 1999).

utilised effectively, these feelings can suggest ways to imagine – and bring into being – a decolonised law school, and more structurally just world.

There are many things that I would change about teaching "Justice, Law, and Human Rights", and I feel that this was only a small move in a decolonial praxis, with many failings. However, it is crucial to engage in this reflective practice regarding our teaching, to keep questioning our role as teachers – and in my case, as a settler teacher and someone trained in European and settler-colonial international law – and to keep critically considering how we can further decolonisation. The lessons from my attempt to decolonise this module can be applied to other modules, including core modules. As scholars have argued in other areas, these discussions must not be siloed into modules (like human rights) which may appear more amendable to discussions of race and colonisation.[74] I hope that by encouraging students to consider what it means to "choose their law"; by introducing them to Indigenous sovereignty, governance, and law in addition to human rights; and by raising the question of British responsibility for colonial and imperial practices, I went some way to offering students a decolonial approach to human rights and jurisprudence. Moreover, I hope that this encouraged students to think of law as a dialogue between multiple legal systems – Indigenous, settler, and colonial – rather than one universal mode, and in this way, we have started a reconceptualisation of the law school as a place where different legal epistemologies can meet.

Acknowledgments

My thanks to Foluke Adebisi for convening such a rich workshop, and for attending to this volume with such care; the reviewers for their comments; Lars Waldorf, with whom I co-taught this module in 2019; Mark McMillan, who has taught me so much; and Fi Belcher for suggesting some relevant literature. All errors, oversights, inabilities, and infelicities, are mine.

Disclosure statement

No potential conflict of interest was reported by the author.

ORCID

Sophie Rigney http://orcid.org/0000-0001-6247-2159

[74]See for example Kim Forde-Mazrui, "Learning Law Through the Lens of Race" (2005) 21(1) Journal of Law and Politics 1, 3, and the citations there referenced; Patricia J Williams, *The Alchemy of Race and Rights* (Harvard University Press 1992); Kimberlé Williams Crenshaw, "Foreword: Toward a Race-Conscious Pedagogy in Legal Education" (1994) 1 National Black Law Journal 1.

Researching colonialism and colonial legacies from a legal perspective

Nandini S. Boodia-Canoo

ABSTRACT

This article focuses on the difficulties encountered by socio-legal researchers in approaching questions on law and history, with particular reference to choosing adequate methodologies. Drawing on her personal experience in researching colonial laws and questions on indigeneity, the author outlines established lines of thought while suggesting new ways of interpreting historical material. An argument is made for applying a legal lens to historical discourses for the unique insight that may be derived from such study. Certain pitfalls in socio-legal research are highlighted, including perspective and positioning in post-colonial scholarship. The author supplies examples from her research on Mauritius as an illustration of how such an approach can be coherently applied to a chosen topic. The article concludes with recommendations for future legal research in the area of colonialism and its legacies.

Introduction

Studying colonialism from a legal perspective does not make for entirely comfortable reading, at least for the lawyer who, like myself, prefers to regard her discipline as a vehicle for justice, progress and welfare in the world. Doctrines of international law, having been extensively developed during the period of colonial expansion, were greatly shaped by the experience, but crucially, the period of colonialism represents an epoch during which violence, oppression and injustice in fact derived their legitimacy from legal rules.[1] This may appear like a travesty, but Christopher Weeramantry believes that such corruption may occur in any area of law when its study and application are divorced from its underlying spirit and moral foundations.[2]

The role of law in colonial rule is an acknowledged one, but appears frequently misconceived in traditional historical discourses. There remains a pronounced preoccupation with the "effectiveness" of law, which more often than not has been deemed inadequate by historians.[3] At the same time, law itself is predominantly an applied discipline, and for legal practitioners the history of law is only relevant in as far as it may have an impact on the law's current state or future development. Thus, from the view of

[1]Christopher Weeramantry, "The Grotius Lecture Series" (1999) 14 American University International Law Review 1515.

[2]ibid 1557.

[3]See Matthew Craven, "Between Law and History: The Berlin Conference of 1884-1885 and the Logic of Free Trade" (2015) 3 London Review of International Law 31.

both historians and lawyers, an in-depth study of colonial laws may be considered a questionable endeavour.

These observations notwithstanding, I believe that a deeper understanding of the long shadow cast by colonialism may be achieved by an exploration through a legal lens. It is submitted that such research is valuable precisely because it involves a consideration of both law and history. Such a scholar is not a legal historian in the usual sense. Instead, the role is more accurately described as "lawyer-historian", because the attempt is to reframe relevant historical events as legal processes as a way of gaining deeper insight into the underlying dynamics of the time.

In the pursuit of such knowledge, scholars may find themselves facing a number of challenges: methodological, theoretical as well as epistemological. Drawing on my own experiences of conducting legal research into colonial history, the following presents an investigation into the relevant concepts and processes which I believe need to be addressed when engaging in such scholarship. This is presented in two parts. In Part I, the focus of this article will be on methodology. For a lawyer looking at history, the "how" is a critical choice, influencing the "what" of her research long before the first findings are made.

The article proceeds in Part II with a case study based on the research I conducted into the colonial laws of Mauritius,[4] a country which may be considered a veritable laboratory for testing and experimenting with theories of colonialism given its distinct history. Some of my findings are included here, not as a full illustration of the methodology I propose (which would be beyond the scope of this publication), but rather to provide an example of the contemporary relevance of legal colonial research and its application beyond a narrow national context.

Part I

The question of methodology in socio-legal research

> No method can protect us from our limitations and our mistakes.
>
> When we speak to the next generation we must be frank in admitting our shortcomings,
>
> while describing what, against all odds, we had been trying to do.[5]

From the beginning the main challenge for me has been to straddle the line between history and law. This has been perfectly summarised by socio-legal scholars Catherine Fisk and Robert Gordon who found their work critiqued and were led to introspection:

> Can we make causal claims? What kind? Should we try? More broadly: What should we study? How much and what kind of study of the "social" is desirable or necessary? What is the "social" and how can we distinguish it from "law"? When legal historians go into the archive, what should we read and how should we interpret the papers we find there? Should we even be in the archive at all? At the most extreme, what is "history" and what is "law"?[6]

---

[4]Nandini Boodia-Canoo, "Assembling a Nation – Law, Labour and Identities in 19th Century Mauritius" (PhD thesis, SOAS University of London 2017).

[5]Carlo Ginzburg, "Our Words, and Theirs: A Reflection on the Historian's Craft, Today" in Susanna Fellman and Marjatta Rahikainen (eds), *Historical Knowledge: In Quest of Theory, Method and Evidence* (Cambridge Scholars Publishing 2012) 116.

[6]Catherine L Fisk and Robert W Gordon, "'Law As . . .': Theory and Method in Legal History" (2011) 1 UC Irvine Law Review 519, 522.

I have asked myself each and every of these questions, and to find they are common to other scholars in the field has been reassuring. Given that law infuses every conceivable part of life, the potential intersections with other disciplines are many and varied. As every intersection adds further dimensions and elements to be considered, such studies do not fit neatly in previously established theoretical frameworks. Correspondingly, any chosen methodology may appear unorthodox. These issues notwithstanding, it is submitted here that law can and does make a valuable methodological contribution. Law provides a particular technique, a process, which focuses on specificity and analysis.[7] Herein lies law's unique offering. The conclusion reached by Fisk and Gordon is therefore heartening: "In matters of theory and method, the possibilities for sociolegal history are as many as can be imagined."[8]

Legal and historical sources

Salient events of the past which have shaped society in fundamental ways frequently tend to be viewed as historical occasions of political significance. In essence however they often are legal processes – particularly where colonial developments are concerned. Whether we are referring to the abolition of slavery, the introduction of alternative forms of labour, or colonisation and eventual decolonisation more broadly, all of these are in effect legal transitions. The value of legal analysis however is not always easily recognised.

In appraising various sources for historical research on slavery, Mauritian historian Vijaya Teelock appears to discount the usefulness of legal sources and states that "the laws relating to slavery and from slave period can be examined but they do not necessarily reflect the actual practice on slavery".[9] That is a correct assessment, and true of any study of law which focuses purely upon the formalities of the legal code. What then constitutes a useful source? In considering what may and what may not amount to historical evidence, R.G. Collingwood uses the example of Roman pottery to explain that it acquires its status of "evidence" not because of the intention of the maker, but because of the researcher's view of it.[10] Similarly, legal sources may become "historical evidence" when scholars deem them as such. The question thus is not whether laws amount to evidence, but rather, what are laws evidence of?

Taking the example of slavery and addressing the above criticism, it is submitted that the lawyer tends to seek a different insight from that of the historian. It is true that a study of the relevant laws and regulations is unlikely to yield much insight into the practice of slavery. However, what such research is capable of showing is on what basis certain customs came into being, or why the practice came to take the specific form it did, as well as what kinds of contestation might have surrounded it as an institution. At its most basic, an examination of the law does reveal explicitly accepted parameters of behaviour, reflecting dominant thought and policy of the time, with provisions designed to measure and control social conduct. A conscious breach would have come at some social or political cost – not necessarily an overriding one in all cases, but a cost, nevertheless. In order to understand an institution such as slavery then, one has to understand the complex relationship between the political, economic and legal

---

[7]Roger Cotterrell, "Law in Social Theory and Social Theory in the Study of Law" in Austin Sarat (ed), *The Blackwell Companion to Law and Society* (Blackwell Publishing 2004).

[8]Fisk and Gordon (n 6) 541.

[9]Vijayalakshmi Teelock, *A Select Guide to Sources on Slavery in Mauritius* (African Cultural Centre 1995) 10.

[10]RG Collingwood, *The Idea of History* (rev edn, with lectures 1926–1928, Clarendon Press 1994) 12.

dimensions of the institution, and how a certain calculating conduct may dispose itself at moments to formal compliance with the rule of law, and at moments to its utter disregard. What this recommends therefore, is an approach to the legal sources that understands the law to be something that can be approached strategically and deliberately, weighing the price of compliance or non-compliance against other social advantages and disadvantages.

In line with recent scholarship that no longer views law as imposed upon the colonised, but rather sees it as a system which was available to be utilised and accessed by all participants to a greater or lesser extent in the colonial setting,[11] it is submitted that law forms a valuable source of historical inquiry, supporting the argument for extending the conception of law beyond that of a mere facilitator and enabler of the imperial project.

Law and history

As research concerned with the processes of legal change in history, it might well be asked how therefore this type of inquiry as described above sits within the field of legal history. David Ibbetson has set out the traditional demarcations in this area, which he refers to as *external* and *internal*.[12] In simple terms, *external legal history* relates to how law operates in its social and economic setting, while *internal legal history* is more focused on the law itself.

I would argue that my approach combines both aspects, but ultimately transcends them: if legal history is commonly concerned with placing law and legal issues within a historical context, my attempt here is to provide a legal contextualisation of history and historical issues. Therefore, to consider the kind of scholarship I have described as "legal history" may be misleading. It is less an historical analysis of law, than a legal analysis of history.

To the extent that it is an inquiry informed by a particular contemporary agenda, it may be seen to run against the protocols of historical scholarship – both in the sense that it risks falling into anachronism, and as Carlo Ginzburg puts it, may mean that we only find "what we are looking for – and nothing else".[13] The question of anachronism will be addressed below, but before doing so, it is worth pausing on the anxiety that Ginzburg expresses here about the ability to step out of a contemporary consciousness when writing about the past.

The past and narrative history

It has been said that in historiography, studying the historian becomes as much a task as studying the history.[14] Keith Jenkins has written widely on history as a discipline and highlights one of the major fallacies in general understanding, namely the pervasive belief that "history" and "the past" are the same.[15] As elucidated by Jenkins, this is incorrect, for the past comes to us already in the form of a story, a narrative.[16] Drawing on David Lowenthal's work,[17] he identifies three problem areas

---

[11]Shaunnagh Dorsett and John McLaren, "Laws, Engagements and Legacies" in Shaunnagh Dorsett and John McLaren (eds), *Legal Histories of the British Empire: Laws, Engagements and Legacies* (Routledge 2014).

[12]David Ibbetson, "What Is Legal History a History Of?" in Andrew Lewis and Michael Lobban (eds), *Law and History* (Oxford University Press 2004).

[13]Ginzburg (n 5) 113.

[14]Roger Spalding and Christopher Parker, *Historiography: An Introduction* (Manchester University Press 2007).

[15]Keith Jenkins, *Re-Thinking History* (Routledge 2003) 7.

[16]ibid 11.

[17]David Lowenthal, *The Past Is a Foreign Country* (Cambridge University Press 1985).

along the history/past dichotomy: epistemological, methodological and ideological. Jenkins identifies the first issue as "epistemological fragility", since not only can the totality of the past not be discerned, it consists in fact of a number of situations and events. Therefore, any account is "inevitably a personal construct, a manifestation of the historian's perspective as a 'narrator'".[18]

This links to Jenkins' second issue, that of methodology, and the general problem of constructing "stories" out of mere fragments of the past. The creation of narratives has been extensively discussed by Hayden White. White ponders that the narrative, while a natural choice of communication, is of ambiguous quality, since it represents both content and form.[19] Moreover, it is employed not exclusively in history, but also in what he calls "non-historical" settings. According to White, "[t]he fact that narrative [...] predominates in both mythic and fictional discourse makes it suspect as a manner of speaking about 'real' events".[20] In this respect, White believes the dichotomy involved is one not of truth and falsehood, but of reality and imagination. His reflections on the subject however appear consciously circular, for he concludes that in any instance, the past cannot be represented in any way other than "imaginary", and wonders whether the final question regarding narratives may actually hinge on "the function of imagination in the production of a specifically human truth".[21]

White's contemplations on the subject serve to further underline the important influence exerted by the author of any historical account. Ann Rigney elucidates it clearly in her argument, that through their choices of what and how to present, historians shape an account, and "in the process, [...] add something to the information they have garnered, [...] a narrative logic that the empirical data did not possess in itself".[22] Rigney goes further to say: "The fact that this emplotment of events is a constructive activity, however, should not be taken to mean that is necessarily fraudulent or valueless. On the contrary: narrating history is the royal way to understanding how events occur the way they do. Knowledge, like a cooked meal, is made, not found."[23]

Carlo Ginzburg argues that, to begin with, the initial questions in historical inquiries are inevitably anachronistic. It is the research process which modifies the original query and provides answers expressed in the subject's language.[24] Thus there exists an inherent tension and divergence between modern vocabulary and its previous meanings. According to Ginzburg, the choice appears to be either to employ original terminology, which risks concealing transformations in understanding, or to apply an altogether new terminology. Neither seems entirely satisfactory. Ginzburg suggests that this "intrinsic weakness", namely a language that is shared yet liable to different interpretations, be countered by the application "of a rigorous vocabulary".[25] The

[18]Jenkins (n 15) 14. This view is echoed in Thomas Skouteris' study on the place of history in international law, see Thomas Skouteris, "Engaging History in International Law" in D Kennedy and JM Beneyto (eds), *New Approaches to International Law: The European and the American Experiences* (TMC Asser Press 2012).

[19]Hayden V White, *The Content of the Form: Narrative Discourse and Historical Representation* (Johns Hopkins University Press 1987) ch 2.

[20]ibid 57.

[21]ibid.

[22]Ann Rigney, "History as Text: Narrative Theory and History" in Nancy Partner and Sarah RI Foot (eds), *The SAGE Handbook of Historical Theory* (SAGE Publications Ltd 2013) 190.

[23]ibid.

[24]Ginzburg (n 5) 108.

[25]ibid 99.

issue identified by Ginzburg is subtle and in practice not easily addressed. His desire for a "rigorous vocabulary" appears to call for the provision of clear definitions, thus creating certainty by applying a fixed meaning to the terminology in question. Yet the rigidity inherent in definitions may be regarded as detrimental to the understanding of historical development, which by nature is a process. By way of example, one such term requiring clarification is "slavery". Ostensibly clear in meaning, the term has been used differently at the beginning of the nineteenth century, post-abolition, during the indenture period (also described as "new slavery"), or indeed now in the twenty-first century as evident in the British Modern Slavery Act 2015. To address the problematic issue of language, it is suggested that scholarship should attempt to locate the meaning of salient terms within their time, but be also attentive to the way in which those terms themselves may change, or vary from one context to the next.

Anne Orford takes the issue one stage further in arguing that historical and legal enquiries have fundamentally different objectives.[26] She questions the feasibility of this obligation to avoid anachronism in the legal arena, asserting that "[l]aw and history stand on the opposite sides of the dividing line between present obligations and archaic traditions".[27] She notes, in that context that "[t]he self-imposed task of today's contextualist historians is to think about concepts in their proper time and place – the task of international lawyers is to think about how concepts move across time and space".[28]

It is submitted that the concern of colonial research is not necessarily to impute to the agents and actors within the account a contemporary sensibility, but understand them in their own terms, by reference to the currents of thought pervading at the time. A further point to observe here is that the main danger may not be that of projecting the present on the past, but of an inability to shake off a past that may be seen to envelop the present.

Western historiography and Eurocentrism

It has become evident that authorship, and in particular the writer's cultural background, significantly colours how certain eras of history are presented, with emphasis, focus and concerns shifting strikingly.[29] Linda Alcoff endorses this point quite emphatically when explaining that a person's location (that is, their social location or identity) affects the "truth" and "meaning" of their discourse, and in fact may give or take authority in respect to what is being stated.[30] She goes so far as to assert that "what is said turns out to change according to who is speaking and who is listening".[31]

Gayatri Chakravorty Spivak, in her seminal essay, makes the indicting assertion that even critical thinkers (such as Michel Foucault and Gilles Deleuze) are complicit in reinforcing hegemonic power divisions through their inability to divorce a Western perspective from their discourse.[32] She describes the fundamental Eurocentrism of

[26]Anne Orford, "The Past as Law or History? The Relevance of Imperialism for Modern International Law" (2012) IILJ Working Paper 2012/2.
[27]ibid 2.
[28]ibid.
[29]Compare for example Saroja Sundararajan, *From Bondage to Deliverance: Indentured Labour in Mauritius and British Guiana* (Allied Publishers 2006) with Richard B Allen, *Slaves, Freedmen and Indentured Laborers in Colonial Mauritius* (Cambridge University Press 2006).
[30]Linda Alcoff, "The Problem of Speaking for Others" [1991] Cultural Critique 5, 6–7.
[31]ibid 12.
[32]Gayatri Chakravorty Spivak, "Can the Subaltern Speak?" in Patrick Williams and Laura Chrisman (eds), *Colonial Discourse and Post-Colonial Theory: A Reader* (Columbia University Press 1994).

situating Europe as "Self" and the subaltern as "Other" as "the epistemic violence of imperialism", a pitfall not truly overcome but merely ignored by intellectuals in their study of history.[33] Spivak believes Foucault's genuine interest in the politics of the oppressed actually serves to obscure the special position he grants the (European) Self.[34] Thus she favours Jacques Derrida, who has identified "the European Subject's tendency to constitute the Other as marginal to ethnocentrism" and regards this susceptibility as the central difficulty "with all logocentric and [...] grammatological endeavours".[35]

This is a theme that is taken up by Dipesh Chakrabarty who, problematically enough, brings the historical method itself into account. In the latter context, he directs his attention towards historicism, arguing that as a theory of history it in fact enabled European hegemony in the nineteenth century.[36] According to Chakrabarty, the historicist notion that certain concepts such as capitalism and modernity spread from Europe to the rest of the world over time, reinforced the concept of a "first in Europe, then elsewhere" view, thus placing non-European people in a perpetual state of "not yet". This is similar to what James Blaut has termed "Eurocentric diffusionism".[37] At its heart is the perception that European modernisation was the result of intrinsic qualities rather than any interaction with the rest of the world. Blaut explains that if we take this assumption as correct (as he asserts many scholars do), other assumptions follow: if the foundations of modernity are European, colonialism was not essential for Europe's progress. If colonialism was not essential, it cannot have been exploitative and destructive. If it was not destructive, it must have been beneficial.[38]

This notion of past or present European superiority is generally simply labelled Eurocentrism. According to Blaut, its removal however is more difficult than merely eliminating such attitudes, because it contains beliefs that are deemed empirical reality or facts, therefore remaining unquestioned and even perpetuated by otherwise unprejudiced European scholars.[39]

Bill Ashcroft, Gareth Griffin and Helen Tiffin take up this point by defining "Eurocentrism" as "[t]he conscious or unconscious process by which Europe and European cultural assumptions are constructed or assumed to be, the normal, the natural, or the universal".[40] These ideas require further exploration, but for the current purposes of contemplating historical sources, the scholars' definition highlights the fact that reference points of many discourses have remained indeed unchallenged European. Cartography hereby presents a perfect example. The creation of maps was an important aspect of colonial and post-colonial practice. However maps and mapping have established geographical standards of contemporary relevance in a world which not only places Europe in the middle and at the top, but makes it the norm and other areas a deviation.[41] Yet these conceptualisations have largely remained the standard of any

---

[33]ibid 84.
[34]ibid 87.
[35]ibid 89.
[36]Dipesh Chakrabarty, *Provincializing Europe: Postcolonial Thought and Historical Difference* (Princeton University Press 2000) 7.
[37]See James M Blaut, *The Colonizer's Model of the World: Geographical Diffusionism and Eurocentric History* (Guilford Press 1993).
[38]ibid 2.
[39]ibid 9.
[40]Bill Ashcroft, Gareth Griffiths and Helen Tiffin, *Post-Colonial Studies: The Key Concepts* (Routledge 2000) 90.
[41]ibid 31–34.

geopolitical discourse. As per Ashcroft and others: "The definition of cultures as tropical in a world where temperate is the norm, or as densely populated or thinly populated, or as resource rich or poor, are essential discriminations upon which a practice of exploitation or control can be erected."[42]

Highlighting perspective

Following this observation of a predisposition to Eurocentrism in modern Western historiography, the question arises as to how this may be effectively avoided, particularly when discussing the process of colonisation. In an attempt to explain how one account of history may become established as normative, Gayatri Spivak ventures into an analysis. She feels the need to open with a disclaimer, almost apologetically, as the example she chooses (British codification of Hindu law) may be regarded as a "nostalgic investigation of the lost roots of my own identity", she says, given her Indian background.[43] Spivak admits her motivations are complex, but asserts that the main aim of her endeavour is to reveal the "positivist-idealist variety of such nostalgia". Alongside language skills and personal experience, she believes that her particular circumstances provide her with "a *sense* of the historical canvass",[44] the value of which however she does not elaborate upon. Spivak thus does not reject the idea of nostalgia, but concedes that "a nostalgia for lost origins can be detrimental to the exploration of social realities within the critique of imperialism".[45] I do not subscribe to the notion that a personal nexus to a subject necessarily involves "nostalgia", whether of the positivist-idealist type or any other kind. While such a link may provide the author with a distinct perspective, it is neither a weakness nor a strength by itself. Rather, it is an ability to provide a specific insight with certain sensibilities observed. It becomes thus a question of the quality of the contribution, not in terms of its standard, but with respect to its attributes. Sentimentality, if at all present, does not automatically affect the rigour of the investigation.

Dipesh Chakrabarty is another scholar who feels the need to state his personal circumstances, providing the reader with details of his cultural and educational background, within the very first pages of his seminal work.[46] As an equally non-white scholar, I cannot but question the intention for doing this. The value of certain acknowledgements in the context of colonial studies notwithstanding, the question arises as to what purpose does this kind of self-identification serve? After all, a similar statement if made by a white scholar would appear rather peculiar. Additionally, for scholars this kind of declaration is usually obsolete, given their frequently non-western name. It is submitted that such identification serves mainly two purposes: either it is an apology along the lines given by Spivak, whereby the author seeks to perform an act of contrition for their interest in a particular area, pre-empting the accusation of "nostalgia" if their expertise is in any way linked to their background, or, more shrewdly perhaps, it is to derive greater authority by demonstrating the author is less privileged,

[42]ibid 33.
[43]Spivak (n 32) 76.
[44]ibid (emphasis in original).
[45]ibid 87.
[46]Dipesh Chakrabarty, *Provincializing Europe: Postcolonial Thought and Historical Difference* (Princeton University Press 2007) 4.

yet an "insider" to the topic, and thus more knowledgeable and with a greater entitlement to speak.

Benjamin Zachariah makes this point emphatically in his essay on Postcolonial Theory. He states: "There is [...] a tendency for the structure of arguments to reduce speakers or writers to their origins, in a manner reminiscent of forms of stereotyping and essentialisation that, it has been argued, are a feature of colonial thought."[47] He questions Spivak's rationalisation of the coloniser's attempt to speak for the subaltern, stating: "... one of her central lines of argument – 'white man saves brown woman from brown man' was her pithy summary of the claim. Which of course left open the question why 'brown elite woman' speaking for 'brown subaltern woman' was a more legitimate form of representation."[48]

This is a question which every ethnic scholar needs to ask him/herself. As explained previously, a personal nexus merely confers a specific point of view, which is not inherently more legitimate or qualitatively superior. There may be an appearance of, or even overt claim to, greater legitimacy, but that is fallacious. Ginzburg makes an interesting observation which is relevant in this context, when analysing what he deems "traps" in historiography: "empathy and ventriloquism".[49] Ginzburg believes a dangerous distortion is created when historians ascribe modern language and categories to the subjects "by assuming the transparency of the actors".[50] Ethnic scholars may arguably be more prone to this, particularly if they have personal links to the subject in question. According to Ginzburg, these pitfalls can be avoided by preserving the contrast between personal interpretation and the information gathered through evidence. As discussed previously however, any digest of information gathered *is* personal interpretation. Even the simple reproduction of data is dependent upon choices based on value judgements made by an author. It is submitted that what is required is an awareness of such tendencies and a conscious rejection of the assumption that the interpretation of any event is obvious, or, especially in the case of ethnic scholars, that its meaning is beyond argument.

Part II

Case study: an example of researching colonial legacies in a multi-ethnic world

Mauritius, a collection of islands in the Indian Ocean commonly referred to in the singular form, has been the focus of my initial research on colonial legacies. Mauritian society presents an amalgam of different cultures and ethnicities, each seeking to protect its interests and jockeying for power, an enduring feature of life on this multi-ethnic island which effectively began in the nineteenth century, when first slaves from the African continent and then indentured labourers from India were imported in support of the colonial project.

The history of Mauritius provides a case study which illustrates issues of relevance beyond the island's own context. In a world where migration, globalisation and multiculturalism are the norm, yet present a source of heightened tension and disquietude,

---

[47] Benjamin Zachariah, "Postcolonial Theory and History" in Nancy Partner and Sarah Rl Foot (eds), *The SAGE Handbook of Historical Theory* (SAGE Publications Ltd 2013) 379–380.
[48] ibid 385 (footnote omitted).
[49] Ginzburg (n 5) 109.
[50] ibid.

the study of multi-ethnic societies is to be encouraged. Frequently, however, a certain hesitance in addressing such concerns is observable in the public discourse, and Mauritius is no exception.

The problem may lie with the notion of "race" itself. Yasmin Gunaratnam points out that researching the concept is fraught with difficulties because it is fundamentally a political and social construct.[51] Citing the definition provided by Stuart Hall, who states that while "race" claims difference on genetic and biological grounds, the idea of "ethnicity" is based in cultural and religious markers, Gunaratnam observes that the two terms nevertheless tend to be used interchangeably. She endorses however Hall's notion, which regards biological and cultural differentiation not as two distinctive discourses, but rather as two strands of racism.[52] I would agree with this conceptualisation. The Mauritian context shows that a strict interpretation of either concept is not applicable, which is why the focus in this research is on "identities", manufactured as they were, during the colonial period. The question of race and ethnicity in Mauritius remains a pervasive one; however, the two concepts are inextricably linked. To say that Mauritians feel divided only by ethnicity would ignore the fact that race consciousness is very much alive, with the idea of "racial purity" within communities continuing to persist to a certain extent.

Racism is a topic that is as relevant in Mauritius today as it was 200 years ago. In analysing the concept, Margaret Davies explains that racism need not involve conscious or even unconscious bias, but rather is perpetrated through symbols and values that can be institutional or individual.[53] Hereby, drawing on Richard Delgado's work, she observes that: "ideas about race are reinforced and made real by material factors such as slavery and other forms of exploitation, as well as by general social disadvantage".[54] This accurately describes the issue of race in Mauritius. Indo- and Afro-Malagasy Mauritians combined represent 95% of the population today.[55] Among them, they share a heritage that includes colonial exploitation in different forms. Nevertheless, contemporary Mauritius seems to view colonialism through a romanticised lens.

Names of influential figures in Mauritian history are ubiquitous in institutions of everyday life, as is the popularity of "colonial-style" architecture, even for modern buildings. An example may be provided by considering the use of one particular name. The early transformation of Mauritius under the leadership of French Governor Mahé de Labourdonnais certainly allows him some claim to the title of "real founder of the colony", as bestowed by local historians.[56] The Governor is commemorated in various ways in Mauritius, including a large statue in the capital city Port Louis, with prominent establishments, including a high-achieving school and a luxury hotel, bearing his name. The name Labourdonnais is synonymous with prestige in modern

---

[51] Yasmin Gunaratnam, *Researching "Race" and Ethnicity: Methods, Knowledge and Power* (SAGE Publications 2003) 4.

[52] ibid 5. See also Stuart Hall, "The Multi-Cultural Question" in Barnor Hesse (ed), *Un/settled Multiculturalisms: Diasporas, Entanglements, Transruptions* (Zed Books Ltd 2000).

[53] Margaret Davies, *Asking the Law Question* (Law Book Company; Sweet & Maxwell 1994).

[54] ibid, citing Richard Delgado, "Two Ways to Think about Race: Reflections on the Id, the Ego, and Other Reformist Theories of Equal Protection" (2001) 89 Georgetown Law Journal 2279 317.

[55] Indo-Mauritian 68%, Creole 27%, Sino-Mauritian 3%, Franco-Mauritian 2%, see Index Mundi, "Mauritius Demographics Profile 2014" <www.indexmundi.com/mauritius/demographics_profile.html> accessed 8 December 2014.

[56] See Anand Mulloo, "Isle de France under Mahé de Labourdonnais" in SN Gayou (ed), *Mauritius under French Administration* (Mahatma Gandhi Institute 1982) 6–7.

Mauritius, but while he may be applauded for the early development he oversaw, he was also responsible for the large-scale utilisation of slavery on the island. Yet the human cost involved in the initial transformation appears entirely forgotten and remains unquestioned in celebrating the colonist's achievements.

According to Davies, liberal thought encourages "colour-blindness", that is, to ignore appearance and race, and effectively remove it from consciousness.[57] Such an act however, as she observes, merely creates an illusion of equality, because it does not give recognition to real and existing disparities. People of different ethnicities may inhabit the same space, but their experience of it is likely to be divergent. This is accurate of contemporary Mauritius too, as evident from the socio-economic situation. However, given the societal makeup of the island, there was and remains a certain reluctance to discuss race and racism, even among academics. Vijaya Teelock points out that influential figures, including Sir Seewoosagar Ramgoolam[58] felt it unwise, even traumatising for the youth, to include the history of slavery and indentured labour in the school curriculum.[59] The problem arises from the notion that Mauritius has remained sufficiently segregated socially that the descendants of the various groups (colonists, slaves, indentured labourers) may be identifiable by appearance and/or name. Thus it was deemed ill-advised to teach a black child from a poor background about the horrible realities of slavery when he or she is living next to a wealthy white person, who in all likelihood would be the descendant of a slave-owner.[60]

This is further compounded by the fact that, as highlighted by Daniel North-Coombes,[61] division of labour has throughout the history of Mauritius run along racial lines, with "certain racial groups [...] prominent in particular occupations". Consequentially, "appropriate stereotypes were always conveniently manufactured to justify the racially hierarchical employment options prevailing at any one time". A related result of this divide was residential segregation, which notably took place following a severe malaria outbreak in 1866,[62] and which to a certain extent persists to this day. Unsurprisingly, politics have been and continue to be largely divided along religious and racial lines, too.

The issue is thus a delicate one. While the tactic of simply removing the debate from the public discourse cannot be endorsed, a balanced and sensitive approach that defuses potential tensions is required.

Beyond national borders: the modern relevance of colonial research

In the context of such research, the question arises: how relevant is colonial history beyond its national borders? Does the analysis undertaken in the Mauritian context have any applicability beyond the island state? Graham Allison and Niall Ferguson have argued for recognition of the subject of "applied history", not as usually defined with reference to the work of archivists or curators, but as a discipline where historians take current issues and trace analogues in the past, in order to suggest possible

---

[57]Davies (n 53) 317.

[58]Sir Seewoosagar Ramgoolam is considered the "father of the nation" in Mauritius, for leading the independence movement and eventually becoming the country's first prime minister.

[59]Vijayalakshmi Teelock, "Bitter Sugar: Slavery and Emancipation in Nineteenth-Century Mauritius" (PhD thesis, University of London (SOAS) 1994).

[60]ibid.

[61]MD North-Coombes, "From Slavery to Indenture: Forced Labour in the Political Economy of Mauritius 1834-1867" in Kay Saunders (ed), *Indentured Labour in the British Empire, 1834-1920* (Croom Helm 1984) 103.

[62]ibid.

interventions and assess likely consequences.[63] Allison and Ferguson admit that historical analogies are not always accurate, nor should applied historians be regarded as "clairvoyants with unclouded crystal balls".[64] However, the scholars do contend that history provides a number of precedents which lend themselves for strategic consideration.

It is submitted that the issues discussed in my "niche" area of research find renewed relevance in the context of migrant workers in the Middle East. The International Labour Organization (ILO) claims that the ratio of migrant to domestic workers is among the highest in the Arab States region, with migrants in the Gulf States accounting for over 10% of all migrants globally.[65] The plight these workers has reignited the discourse of "slavery" in the twenty-first century, and a closer examination of their conditions reveals parallels which are indeed highly reminiscent of indenture migration in Mauritius in the nineteenth century. The similarities are in many instances striking, suggesting that certain circumstances and conditions yield similar outcomes, however remote in time and space the situations in question may be.

Indian labourers recruited to work on the sugar plantations in nineteenth-century Mauritius confronted a number of exploitative practices,[66] starting with the recruitment process. Once on the island, they had to adapt to a society which initially had no experience of a labour system other than slavery. Even as the indenture system developed and eventually became state-regulated in a move which was expected to prevent further abuses, the laws passed were highly restrictive, designed to keep the labourers restricted in their movements and bound to their employers for as long as possible, with any breaches of contract on their part attracting criminal punishment.

A 2015 report produced by the International Organization for Migration (IOM) investigated the conditions experienced by the thousands of migrants from sub-Saharan Africa, South Asia and South-East Asia who travel to the Middle East and North Africa for employment.[67] The workers in question are employed predominantly in the construction, agricultural and manufacturing sectors, as well as in domestic roles.[68] Crucially, it is pointed out that many migrants are aware of the many human rights abuses and labour law breaches, but this does not act as a deterrent to their decision. The report provides a summary of grievances which is surprisingly reminiscent of the conditions suffered by slaves and indentured labourers.

The report argues that the workers are highly vulnerable as a result of being employed in roles that isolate them either physically (as in a domestic setting) or geographically (such as on farms). A further contributory factor is identified in the discrimination migrant workers suffer from, which it is argued is apparent "in particularly paternalistic attitudes resulting in denial of freedom of movement". "Protection deficits" are said to lie in the

---

[63] Graham Allison and Niall Ferguson, "Why the U.S. President Needs a Council of Historians" *The Atlantic* (2016) <www.theatlantic.com/magazine/archive/2016/09/dont-know-much-about-history/492746/> accessed 23 November 2016.

[64] ibid.

[65] International Labour Organization, "Labour Migration (Arab States)" <www.ilo.org/beirut/areasofwork/labour-migration/lang--en/index.htm> accessed 7 February 2017.

[66] Boodia-Canoo (n 4).

[67] Samantha McCormack, Jacqueline Larsen and Hana Husn, "The Other Migrant Crisis" (International Organization for Migration 2015) <https://publications.iom.int/system/files/pdf/other_migrant_crisis.pdf> accessed 11 June 2016.

[68] ibid 1.

criminalisation of workers who breach their contracts by escaping, as well as shortcomings in legislation and law enforcement more generally.[69]

A White Paper by the ILO, examining in particular the issues arising from labour migration through the "Asia-Arab States corridor", underlines the transnational role of recruitment agencies in rendering the migrant's position vulnerable.[70] The Paper highlights their "fraudulent practices", which reportedly include deception with respect to the nature of work, as well as placing the prospective worker in a kind of debt bondage through exorbitant recruitment fees and charges, resulting in contract substitution and human trafficking.[71] The Paper also criticises the collusion of agents in the origin and destination countries which, it is claimed, is to a large extent responsible for the exploitation of workers.

A similar set-up underpinned early emigration from India to Mauritius.[72] Both Indian and Mauritian police turned a blind eye towards breaches in regulations, amounting to a transnational failure in enforcing legislation. Deception in the recruitment process as well as kidnap and other types of coercion were frequently reported. The "advance" payment of wages (eventually prohibited) operated to place the new worker in debt before even starting service, since it resulted in no remittances for the first six months after arrival. All this led to placing the new migrant in a highly vulnerable position.

A more personal insight into the conditions of migrants in the Gulf States has been provided by Ghaith Abdul-Ahad.[73] Describing the squalid labour camps around the Emirati cities of Dubai and Abu Dhabi, Abdul-Ahad's interviews with construction workers (of notably South-Asian origin, meaning Indian, Pakistani and Sri Lankan) provide a picture which appears to have been taken straight from the nineteenth century.

The majority of the workers not only were illiterate and did not know the content of their contracts, they lived an existence separate from the rest of society, spending nearly their entire day on the construction sites. The workers were viewed by locals as "slaves", and integration into the resident communities appears completely barred. Instead, the workers are considered expendable. "They are the cheapest commodity here. Steel, concrete, everything is up, but workers are the same", according to a group of engineers interviewed.[74] The debt incurred in the recruitment process as well as overall low wages renders the workers unable to accumulate sufficient funds to return home, which, in acute cases, may render them entirely destitute.

The effects are not merely problematic for the workers in question. In August 2016, it was reported that Indian diplomats in Saudi Arabia distributed 15 tonnes of emergency aid to thousands of Indian construction workers who found themselves without any means of subsistence or the ability to return to India after being dismissed by their employers, while ministers of the Indian government were having to establish a repatriation plan.[75]

It is clear that weight cannot be placed on the choice of the worker not to engage in such contracts. Whether in the nineteenth century, or the twenty-first, the reality proves for many migrants to be one as articulated by economist Joan Robinson: "The misery of

---

[69]ibid.

[70]Ray Jureidini, *Ways Forward in Recruitment of Low-Skilled Migrant Workers in the Asia-Arab States Corridor* (International Labour Organization 2016) 6–10.

[71]ibid.

[72]Discussed in detail in Boodia-Canoo (n 4).

[73]Ghaith Abdul-Ahad, "'We Need Slaves to Build Monuments'" *The Guardian* (London, 8 October 2008) <www.theguardian.com/world/2008/oct/08/middleeast.construction> accessed 11 June 2016.

[74]ibid.

[75]Amy Kazmin and Simeon Kerr, "India Sends Aid to Stranded Workers in S Arabia" *Financial Times* (London, 2 August 2016) 6.

being exploited by capitalists is nothing compared to the misery of not being exploited at all."[76] Consent, therefore, cannot be allowed to be employed as a defence.

The view that consent does not negate the existence of a state of exploitation is echoed in the new British legislation, the Modern Slavery Act 2015.[77] Creating offences with respect to holding or placing a person in "slavery, servitude and forced or compulsory labour",[78] as well as "human trafficking",[79] in both instances the "consent" to the situation in question is deemed irrelevant.[80] While section 3 of the Act provides a broad definition of the concept of "exploitation", particularly in the context of service provision under subsection 5, slavery, servitude and forced or compulsory labour are defined by reference to Article 4 of the European Convention on Human Rights.

Crucially, Article 4 does not provide a definition for either slavery or servitude, whereas the prohibition against forced or compulsory labour is subject to several exceptions, notably not covering "any work or service which forms part of normal civic obligations".[81] Thus the legislation, while to be welcomed for introducing a new level of accountability and transparency,[82] raises, or perhaps more accurately, reintroduces, questions on the nature of slavery and servitude. A precise definition of slavery is still elusive. By the same token, a definition of "freedom" in the context of labour remains open to debate, for what is considered "free labour" may also be called "wage slavery".[83]

Based on my research, I do not consider the central issue to be one of "free" or "unfree" labour, whatever these terms are taken to signify. While "slavery" and "freedom" will no doubt continue to be concepts of debate, I would suggest that "exploitation" is a more tangible concept, and more easily recognisable independent of historical setting, taking similar shape, with potentially similar effects, across time and space.

Conclusion

As has been demonstrated in this brief overview, investigations conducted with respect to the colonial history of a geographically small and insular state contain insights relevant to international scholarship.

I hope the reader will have gained both tools and inspiration to engage in legal colonial research through the ideas presented in this paper. Part of my aim in pursuing this kind of work is to demonstrate that colonial legacies present a shared history within society. Issues of racism and the meaning of freedom raise questions that are inextricably linked to the past. They must be addressed through a discourse that is aware of its epistemological roots, yet applicable to contemporary challenges. The modern relevance of such research should not be underestimated, whether in Mauritius, Britain, or indeed any other country.

---

[76] Quoted by Tim Harford, "The Sweatshop Dilemma" *FT Magazine* (22 October 2016) 45.
[77] Passed 26 March 2015.
[78] Section 1.
[79] Section 2.
[80] See s 1(5) and s 2(2) respectively.
[81] Article 3(4)(d).
[82] Section 54 of the Act requires commercial organisations with a certain turnover to provide annual compliance statements publicly.
[83] Stanley L Engerman, "Introduction" in Stanley L Engerman (ed), *Terms of Labor: Slavery, Serfdom and Free Labor* (Stanford University Press 1999) 2.

Acknowledgments

The author would like to thank Dr Foluke Adebisi for her support and encouragement in the publication of this article.

Disclosure statement

No potential conflict of interest was reported by the author.

ORCID

Nandini S. Boodia-Canoo http://orcid.org/0000-0003-3567-2483

"Why is it my problem if they don't take part?" The (non) role of white academics in decolonising the law school

Nick Cartwright and T.O. Cartwright

ABSTRACT
The title of this paper is based on a question we were asked by a white colleague at a staff development session we were delivering. It is our problem because we are implicated in creating and perpetuating a colonised law curriculum. The focus of this paper is on what the role of white academics is in decolonising the law school; we contend that we cannot decolonise the curriculum if we do not first decolonise ourselves. This paper is grounded in critical race theory and concurs with Paulo Freire's position that the oppressor cannot achieve liberation, this is a role solely for the oppressed. The role of decolonised white academics is, we argue, to work within their own communities to ensure the unconditional surrender of power to oppressed Black communities. This role, including the passivity of white power-holders, is however a complex one but if the transfer of power is not achieved, then an insurgent pedagogy where power is taken would be a just course of action.

Introduction: "Why is it my problem if they don't take part?"

This paper is based on our understanding of the current state of the educational process in the United Kingdom, its effect on the engagement of students of colour, the urgency of need to have education as the exercise of liberation and the (non)role of white academics on this journey.

We have been delivering staff development sessions at the University of Northampton that focus on students' Black (with a capital "b") identities and the curriculum; the quote that is the title of this article is a direct quote from a participant in one of our sessions. Where we use "Black" with a capital "b" we are referring to the political identity that many people of colour, including those with mixed or Asian heritage, identify, whereas when we use "black" it is to refer to people of Afro-Caribbean heritage. The quote was chosen because it represents an attitude that is common to many of our colleagues, both white and of colour, who seem to subscribe to the view that higher education (HE) either is, or should be, a colour-blind meritocracy where issues of engagement, retention, progression and achievement must necessarily be about merit and not the colour of one's skin.

Meritocracy is a concept about how desert should be calculated. Desert is the state of affairs deserved by the subject as a consequence of something about the subject.[1]

[1] Owen McLeod, "Contemporary Interpretations of Desert: Introduction" in Louis P Pojman and Owen McLeod (eds), *What Do We Deserve: A Reader on Justice and Desert* (OUP 1998) 61–62; Louis P Pojman, *Justice* (Pearson 2006) 21; George Sher, *Desert* (Princeton University Press 1987) 7.

Michael Young, who coined the term in a satirical journal article, expressed it as "I.Q. + effort = merit".[2] In terms of race, arguing there is a meritocracy leads to claims of colour-blindness – literally not being able to even see racial difference. After the civil rights era many Americans claimed that they "do not see race"[3] leading to an attitude described by as "colour-blind racism". As the journalist, broadcaster and author Afua Hirsch reflects, this is also true in modern-day Britain: "In Britain we are taught not to see race. We are told that race does not matter. We have convinced ourselves that if we can contort ourselves into a form of blindness, then issues of identity will quietly disappear."[4] Meritocracy is of course a fallacy in HE where gender, race, sexual orientation, social class and many other factors are influential. This in turn makes colour-blindness a perspective that is difficult to justify; often it is no more than a refusal to see one's own privilege. The belief in a colour-blind meritocracy is an attitude that comes from a colonisation of so much of our view of the world and our students that we ourselves have become colonised.

There have been calls in recent years to "decolonise the curriculum" because the curriculum is not reflective of the diverse communities HE institutions serve in modern Britain. While this change is long overdue, the magnitude of what is required from the HE sector does not seem to be understood.

First, to "decolonise the curriculum", there has to be a general acceptance that the curriculum is colonised and has been for a long time. Secondly, there must be a clear understanding of what "colonisation" means in the context of HE. Thirdly, academics and those who work within the HE environment must recognise and accept their implicit role with creating and perpetuating this colonisation. Finally, we argue that the process of decolonisation must therefore, necessarily, involve an explicit exercise of the decolonising of ourselves because self-decolonisation is a necessary foundation for collective decolonisation. Each of these four points is taken in turn below.

The first issue requires a common understanding of the terminology around the (de) colonisation debate. On 9 March 2015, the Rhodes Must Fall movement was born[5] – the beginning of a popular movement to decolonise the curriculum. At the centre of many of the debates are differing, and sometimes competing, concepts of what colonisation means in the context of the university curriculum. To understand colonisation in the context of the university curriculum it is first necessary to understand what colonisation is in a broader context. Historically colonisation has meant that the answers to certain epistemological and ontological questions were privileged to the extent that rather than being seen to be one perspective they were elevated to the status of irrefutable truths. Rationality was privileged over the emotional. The written record was privileged over the oral tradition. Jurists took Eurocentric ideas of right and just and reframed them as universal human rights. Autonomy was elevated above relational concerns. Kantian deontology became the dominant ideology. History was written, and rewritten, by the victors, and according to critical race pedagogy state-run education became the way in which these perspectives became formalised and taught as "truth". If you knew

---

[2]Michael Young, *The Rise of the Meritocracy*(2nd edn, Routledge 2017) xiii.

[3]Tyrone A Forman, "Color-Blind Racism and Racial Indifference: The Role of Racial Apathy in Facilitating Enduring Inequalities" in Maria Krysan and Amanda E Lewis (eds), *The Changing Terrain of Race and Ethnicity* (Russell Sage Foundation 2004) 45.

[4]Afua Hirsch, *Brit(ish): On Race, Identity and Belonging*(reprint edn, Vintage 2018) 10.

[5]Nick Cartwright, "Universities Should Be Dangerous Places: But Not Yet" (*HuffPost*, 20 January 2017) <www.huffingtonpost.co.uk/nick-cartwright/universities-should-be-da_b_9037050.html> accessed 1 September 2020.

these truths you were educated; if you refuted them you were ignorant, especially if your perspective was emotional or uncodified. This history has informed a dominant ideology which means that all aspects of our everyday lives are colonised and the effect of this is that those who are white, male and straight – to whose advantage this alleged truth has been skewed – are made to feel comfortable, safe and as if everything is right. For those who are other – Black, female (if we take a cis-gender perspective), or queer – this truth is jarring, uncomfortable, as if something is wrong. This is what Peggy McIntosh is explaining when she talks of the invisible knapsacks of privilege and oppression we all carry,[6] or Afua Hirsch refers to as microaggressions.[7] This is what we understand as colonisation.

In relation to the curriculum and colonisation – the second issue – the enlightenment privileged allegedly objective criteria, elevating them to irrefutable truths. The written word became the only respected way to communicate knowledge, expressed in the passive voice. Oral traditions were not regarded as reliable and appropriate academic sources. Rationality was elevated with emotional responses relegated, for no reason other than bias.[8] These allegedly objective criteria become reframed as merit and we are told that any achievements or failures are because of how we measure up against these "objective" criteria – race and gender have nothing to do with it. Meritocracy, we are told is class-less, colour-blind and gender-blind, although the very concepts of merit are classed, racialised, gendered and heteronormative. This leads to an epistemology where what counts as knowledge is tightly defined and those who are allowed to define what counts as knowledge become an ever more homogenous clique. Similarly, we are also faced with an ontology as to what counts as knowing. We must express our autonomous ideas rationally and in an accepted form. There is no room for communal knowing, emotional knowing or non-traditional forms of expression. The anti-histories central to critical race theory (CRT) do not meet these criteria and therefore they have been ignored for too long. CRT grew out of the critical legal studies movement and adopts an ontological relativism and epistemological constructivism in contrast to the objective certainties of the enlightenment. The central elements of CRT are that it views racism as endemic in our legal and social structures, it is deeply critical of the apparent gains made for people of colour through movements like the American civil rights movement, it is critical of liberal claims of meritocracy and colour-blindness, and it focuses on the experiential elements of knowledge and knowing.[9] The enlightenment in contrast, with its binary conceptions of truth and falsehood creates a false dichotomy with which it is almost impossible not to engage – if one expression of reality conflicts with what is accepted as truth then it must necessarily be false. Any space for perspectives, personal truths, or experiential ways of knowing is extinguished. In the context of the law curriculum what counts as knowledge is tightly defined by the white academia, which is the homogenous clique, and we force our students to express their ideas in ways that we prescribe.

---

[6]Peggy McIntosh, "White Privilege: Unpacking the Invisible Knapsack" (*SEED*, 1999) <https://nationalseedproject.org/Key-SEED-Texts/white-privilege-unpacking-the-invisible-knapsack> accessed 1 July 2020.

[7]Hirsch (n 4).

[8]Catriona Mackenzie and Natalie Stoljar, *Relational Autonomy: Feminist Perspectives on Autonomy, Agency, and the Social Self* (OUP 2000).

[9]David Gillborn, "Critical Race Theory and Education: Racism and Anti-Racism in Educational Theory and Praxis" (2006) 27 Discourse: Studies in the Cultural Politics of Education 11.

On the third point – that those of us who work in HE are implicit in perpetuating colonisation – people of colour are as susceptible to colonisation and to peddling myths that perpetuate colonisation as their white counterparts. For example, students of colour are often quick to accept additional skills support and confidence building offered them which is founded in the deficit model of racial difference and we have encountered many academics from minority groups who adopt the attitude of "if I had to struggle, so should they". Whilst colonisation and whiteness are interrelated the connection is not necessary. It is however true that the roles of those who have directly experienced racial oppression are different from the roles of those who have not, and that white academics must adopt a very different position when decolonising the curriculum from their colleagues of colour. Our black, male students are more likely to have encountered the criminal justice system as the subjects of a stop and search than their peers, and certainly than their lecturers, yet this perspective is not in our teaching of the law. Further, the marketisation of education within the UK has led to a perception of students as passive consumers.[10] Paulo Freire describes this as the banking model of education, with us, as lecturers, having access to knowledge that students can withdraw in a transactional way.[11] Freire argues this model of knowledge is oppressive and disempowering. Very little consideration is given to the students' lived experiences, perspectives, or how the content of what is being taught applies to them which generates what Freire describes as "real knowledge".[12] Instead we focus on the transmission of existing dominant ideologies. For example, lecturers use illustrations from their own experiences of getting a mortgage and having a property conveyed either not realising, or not caring, that many of their students will have come from families where home ownership is not the reality. The embracing of the employability agenda seems to make the claim of Marxists that education prepares students to become cogs in the wheels of capitalism truer than ever. Students accept this unquestioningly because right from their reception years they have been conditioned to think that their perspectives and voices are irrelevant to their education, and as lecturers we do not do enough to challenge this. It therefore comes as no surprise that student engagement, particularly as it relates to black students, suffers. Considering the advances in the arts, sciences and technology over the last century, the way we teach, and the power dynamics between teacher and student appears to be almost static: the "sage on the stage" dispensing her wisdom to the humble yet hungry subjects (students) in the hope that they will remember and be able to regurgitate this inauthentic knowledge at a later date.[13] This banking model of knowledge[14] is a form of colonisation and as colonisation destroyed the cultural identities of the colonised, the legacies of which live on, so also our colonised way of learning and teaching destroys our students' identities as active participants in their educational journeys, the ripple effects of which are felt in our classrooms.

According to Freire: "It is only the oppressed who, by freeing themselves, can free their oppressors."[15] This creates a dichotomy both about the role of the oppressor, who has power but lacks the ability to change the power relationship, and about the

[10] Bell Hooks, *Teaching to Transgress* (Routledge 1994) ch 5.
[11] Paulo Freire, *Pedagogy of the Oppressed* (2nd rev edn, Penguin 1996).
[12] ibid ch 2.
[13] ibid 71.
[14] ibid ch 2.
[15] ibid 56.

oppressed who has the ability but not the power. As with all relational power dynamics, it is unusual for power-holders to relinquish the power they wield unless there is something to be gained by so doing. However, in order to create a decolonised curriculum, it is imperative that all power-holders recognise and accept the full effect of colonisation on the current identities of students of colour both as something real and as something that they can never fully understand. They must relinquish power unconditionally, without understanding how it will be wielded, conscious that this may undermine the privilege that gave them this power in the first place. Attempting to gift decolonisation to our students is as patronising as colonisation itself and because it comes from a place where full knowledge is impossible, is doomed to fail. Similarly, relinquishing power with conditions, for carefully defined purposes, is only ever going to be self-serving. Ultimately any project where power is not relinquished will only be an example of what CRT describes as "interest convergence", when giving some benefit to the oppressed is in the interest of the oppressors, historically the Macpherson Report and more recently the Office for Students (OfS) focus on BAME attainment being obvious examples.

Decolonising the curriculum must be a shared project, but it must be led by our students of colour. We as academics become guides who recognise the value of each individual student voice and our classrooms become communities where our students, as active participants in their educational journeys, feel a responsibility to contribute, thereby creating real knowledge and making education the exercise of liberation for both students and academics. Within this project, the role, including the passivity, of white power-holders is a complex one which we now explore.

To address our overarching assertion on self-decolonisation we need to address the following five questions:

(1) What is colonisation?
(2) How is the curriculum colonised?
(3) How am I colonised?
(4) How do we decolonise ourselves?
(5) Why is self-decolonisation necessary to decolonise the curriculum?

However, first it is necessary to examine and contextualise the assertion.

The conversation about the effect colonisation still has on Black people and the way they are perceived is one our society has yet to confront and one that needs to be addressed. The ongoing impact of colonisation controls the identity of the colonised and their descendants and it is so far-reaching that those who have made Britain their home, as either first or subsequent generation immigrants, are met with persistent reminders that they were "othered" as barbaric to allow for a narrative where white saviours first discovered and then civilised them. According to Afua Hirsch,[16] even liberal progressives expect gratitude from the minorities they have supported. Being Black *and* British means adopting an identity but never being able to adopt the privilege that is an integral part of white identities. Decolonisation must therefore be an intentional project beyond the mere passing of time as such; it must be Black led and white power-holders need to be complicit in its realisation if it is to be peaceably achieved.

[16] Hirsch (n 4).

What is colonisation?

This concept is introduced above but requires expanding upon here. British society is one steeped in institutional legacies of slavery and oppression and since these legacies have yet to be properly acknowledged and addressed the identity of Black people within this society is in limbo: "Since, in British thinking, all black people are immigrants and some are illegal, the only thing to do is suspect the lot."[17] For some, this leads to searching for an identity when they are disconnected from a culture that they did not grow up in. They are not fully accepted into the "hostile environment" where those who appear non-white are told to "go home", and the contributions of people of colour are not fully recognised or are written out of history: "traces of black life have been removed from the British past to ensure that blacks are not part of British future".[18] David Olusoga describes his experiences of growing up in England as: "My right, not just to regard myself as a British citizen, but even to be in Britain seemed contested."[19]

Colonisation is not, at least in this context, about removing flags or granting independence. It is about the historical and contemporary issues that have led to the circumstances in which people of colour in Britain live within a colonised environment. The ideology becomes described variously as "British values", "justice", "fairness" or even "universal truth" and is ascribed a status which means to challenge it is "unpatriotic", "political correctness gone mad", and an act of "treachery". The worst of these "traitors" compound their guilt by not being white and therefore are viewed as having only a tangential relationship with Britishness which they are seen to have rejected in an act of gross ingratitude towards their "hosts".

The way history is told is in part to blame for this one-sided concept of "knowing". For instance, the perspective from which Britain's involvement in the scramble for Africa is told in the history books and taught in schools fails to consider the impact partitioning the African continent to suit European imperialist agendas had on the culture and traditions of the African peoples the world over as well as its legacy on their present lived experiences. The description of African peoples as sub-human by seminal philosophers such as David Hume and Immanuel Kant, as well as their display at ethnological expositions highlights the history of subjugation and impassivity in relation to people of colour in Britain. If our history books fail to depict historical facts in their full gore and glory, it comes as no surprise that our enlightenment processes are skewed. It is clear that Kant and his contemporaries were obsessed with finding a scientific explanation for the causes of black skin; however, their obsession was the catalyst for racist persuasions on human diversity, espousing the idea of white supremacy. It is paradoxical that these enlightenment thinkers also adopted the view that there is a universal desire for true enlightenment, freedom and equality. While this may be true, history shows that equality was conceived as equality among people presumed in advance to be equal, hence the justification to treat as unequal those who did not fit within that confined paradigm. The law has unquestioningly accepted this legacy of equality and law schools reinforce it in their learning and teaching strategies.

---

[17] Anon, "Background – British Racism" (Autumn 1981/Winter 1982) 23 Race and Class 232, 243.

[18] John Solomon and others, "The Organic Crisis of British Capitalism and Race: The Experience of the Seventies" in Centre for Contemporary Studies, *The Empire Strikes Back: Race and Racism in 70s Britain* (Hutchinson 1982) 32.

[19] David Olusoga, *Black and British: A Forgotten History* (Pan Books 2017) xv.

How is the curriculum colonised?

As academics we make political decisions in the perspectives that we present to our students, the reading lists we ascribe to our modules and the way we assess our students. We talk about treating our students equally, but we still have huge retention, progression and awarding gaps in favour of white students.[20] We also teach our students to think critically; however, when they challenge oppressive dominant ideologies within HE, their concerns are often dismissed. When the #RhodesMustFall movement challenged Oxford University Chancellor, Chris Patten on the glorification of Rhodes and the omission of the historical truths of black people from the curriculum, his response was that: "if students don't like the 'generosity of spirit' shown to historical figures like Rhodes, they should think about being educated elsewhere".[21] This is symptomatic of the attitude of what we characterise as the "patronising liberal" later in this paper.

The dominant ideology behind educational policy persists as one of colour-blind meritocracy. Critical theorists argue that the rules written by straight, white men privilege them and disadvantage others. Therefore, the formal equality stance of equal treatment has done little to erode the inequalities of outcome we see in pay gaps and educational achievement.

The students' relationships to learning and knowledge and how they perceive knowledge is shaped by their "working identity".[22] The roles and behaviours students adopt are racialised and students make unconscious, or even conscious, choices as to how they wish to be perceived.[23] Devon Carbado and Muti Gulati argue that the working identity that a student has – both how she sees herself and how others see her – affects her experiences of education.[24] If she has a working identity that assimilates whiteness and masculinity then her position in relation to learning and knowledge and the power and privilege this gives her are different from if she has a working identity that incorporates blackness and femininity:

> What *counts* as knowledge, the ways in which it is organized, who is empowered to teach it, what counts as an appropriate display of having learned it, and – just as critically – who is allowed to ask and answer all these questions are part and parcel of how dominance and subordination are reproduced and altered in society.[25]

The meritocratic and colour-blind attitudes discussed above are founded in a view as to what knowledge and learning are which stands in contrast to the views preferred by critical theorists such as Freire[26] that learning and knowledge should be grounded in praxis, specifically a combination of action and reflection.

The purpose of education, Freire argues, is not to understand the circumstances that cause oppression but to change them so that the student can achieve liberation. The

[20] Advance HE, "Degree Attainment Gaps" (2019) <www.advance-he.ac.uk/guidance/equality-diversity-and-inclusion/student-recruitment-retention-and-attainment/degree-attainment-gaps>.

[21] "Patten Criticism of Cecil Rhodes Campaign 'Scandalous'" (*Today*, BBC Radio 4, 14 January 2016) <www.bbc.co.uk/programmes/p03fgfxg>.

[22] Devon W Carbado and Mitu Gulati, *Acting White? Rethinking Race in Post-Racial America* (OUP 2013) 1.

[23] ibid.

[24] ibid.

[25] Michael W Apple, "The Politics of Official Knowledge: Does a National Curriculum Make Sense?" (1993) 95(2) Teachers College Record 222, 222.

[26] Freire (n 11).

banking model of education is oppressive, and the end achieved is domination. Freire proposes instead a model of education for liberation.[27]

College campuses in the US are described as "white spaces"[28] and similar charges have been made of HE institutions in the UK which Heidi Mirza describes as: "complex entrenched institutionalised gendered and classed racial discrimination in British universities".[29] The predominant belief among white Americans is that black people are doing as well as whites, and any differences in outcome are explained by merit, choices or sometimes social class.[30] There are four beliefs that are ascribed to what is described as colour-blind racism:[31] the first is that society is meritocratic, the second that for most, race is something they pay little or no attention to, thirdly that therefore any patterns of inequalities of outcomes for certain racial groups must be because of individual desert or collective cultural reasons, and fourthly that there is therefore no need to act to address the causes of inequalities of outcome.

This colour-blind attitude steeped in a belief that our society is close to being a meritocracy could be argued to underpin British educational policy. If this is true, then it may also be the case we as academics have bought into the ideology of colour-blind meritocracy.

Our students have been exposed to an ideology of education that is grounded in both meritocracy and colour-blind racism and "[a]s a result of this belief system, the true structural, institutional, and societal causes of inequity go unnoticed, and efforts to address these causes are viewed as illegitimate and unnecessary".[32]

The educational institutions that these students will have attended are likely to have been influenced by government policy. Frances Stage and Kathleen Manning map six presumptions that educational institutions make when working with students of colour which reflect the meritocratic and colour-blind attitudes we also experienced in our work.[33] First, it is students of colour that are expected to change to fit the dominant white, Eurocentric culture and not vice versa. Secondly, racial diversity and inclusion is made the responsibility of staff or students of colour. Thirdly, students of colour are expected to share the interests of other students and subjected to criticism when they do not participate or try to organise their own, race-specific groups. Fourthly, students of colour are criticised for their failure to engage with study skills or support sessions, being labelled as lazy or ungrateful. The assumption that underpins this attitude is claimed to be that all students of colour need remedial support. Fifth, the institution adopts the colour-blind stance of offering equal opportunities for all. Finally, the white culture of the institution is assumed to be functioning properly and not in need of any change.

---

[27] ibid ch 2.

[28] Joe R Feagin, Hernan Vera and Nikhita Imani, *The Agony of Education: Black Students at White Colleges and Universities* (Routledge 1996); Paul Kivel, "The Culture of Power" in Frank W Hale Jr (ed), *What Makes Racial Diversity Work in Higher Education: Academic Leaders Present Successful Policies and Strategies* (Stylus 2004); Nirmal Puwar, "Fish in or out of Water: A Theoretical Framework for Race and the Space of Academia" in Ian Law, Deborah Phillips and Lorna Turney (eds), *Institutional Racism in Higher Education* (Trentham Books 2004).

[29] Heidi Safia Mirza, "Racism in Higher Education: 'What Then, Can Be Done?'" in Jason Arday and Heidi Safia Mirza (eds), *Dismantling Race in Higher Education: Racism, Whiteness and Decolonising the Academy* (Palgrave Macmillan 2018) 4.

[30] Forman (n 3).

[31] ibid.

[32] Robert D Reason and Nancy J Evans, "The Complicated Realities of Whiteness: From Color Blind to Racially Cognizant" (2007) 120 New Directions for Student Services 67, 69.

[33] Frances K Stage and Kathleen Manning (eds), *Enhancing the Multicultural Campus Environment: A Cultural Brokering Approach: New Directions for Student Services* (Jossey-Bass 1992).

We conclude in this paper that, as academics, it is impossible to decolonise the curriculum if we do not first decolonise ourselves. Self-decolonisation is the necessary foundation for collective decolonisation. To assess the practicality of decolonising a curriculum, over the past year we have listened to the lived experiences of Black students and academics and related these counter-narratives back to academics through developmental workshops. This is a complex activity as many Black people are not fully aware of the oppression they have suffered or of how to articulate this to an audience that has not shared in their lived experience. Giving someone a voice without having an impact upon what they say is a very difficult task and for many Black people, it is too easy to fall into parroting the myth they are expected to tell of egalitarianism, meritocracy and self-blame. Further, the justifiable anger that is sometimes part of the counter-narrative can antagonise the listener who may already be minded to belittle these experiences. When we used examples of academics mispronouncing non-English names in our sessions one attendee joked that he did not even bother trying to read their names but ignored them; others refused to accept that names are important. Many people of colour will have become used to defensive responses which themselves become a form of micro-aggression, as Reni Eddo-Lodge notes: "I just can't engage with the bewilderment and the defensiveness ..."[34] The identities of Black British people are in fact difficult for anyone to comprehend; they have both a Black identity which is necessarily imbued with historic injustices, although this relates to a geographic space they may have never called home, and a British identity which is viewed with suspicion, as somehow fraudulent because Britishness and whiteness are perceived as necessarily related.

I ('Teleola), as a black woman from Nigeria, found it difficult to understand the plight of Black British students for a number of reasons, which we find are typical of black people from former colonies. First, British education was my first encounter of being treated as intellectually inferior based on skin colour; I still find this bizarre. In Nigeria, I was a member of the dominant racial group so whilst the subject-matter of my education I now know to be problematic because of the parts of colonial history, and especially slavery, that were either reframed or omitted I never felt unable to participate in learning activities. Secondly, I thought Black British students had the advantage of "knowing the ropes" as they unlike me, knew the system. I was moving to a new country so already felt like an outsider; they were home students. I also thought that they had access to funding and opportunities that I had only dreamed of, so my initial perception of the so-called BME attainment gap was that the students who were not doing well were simply lazy, making excuses, had too much choice, or were lacking in aspiration. I felt that if I was able to work hard and succeed despite the obstacles I faced, "they" had no excuse. This myth of meritocracy is perhaps the greatest threat to decolonisation. It assumes that the playing field is level and that hard work guarantees success. It is also an attitude that some of my contemporaries still hold, looking down on Black British students and disowning their experiences, further complicating their identities.

I (Nick), as a white British man, went from an all-white secondary school to a predominantly white and very middle-class university in the mid-1990s. People of colour were not part of my educational experience so the seeds of otherness and even exoticism were already sown. As the first person in my family to go away to university I was allowed to feel like educational opportunities were now more widely

[34] Reni Eddo-Lodge, *Why I'm No Longer Talking to White People About Race* (Bloomsbury 2017) x.

available and that once we had broken in the meritocratic HE system would give us social mobility. During the 1990s the British National Party (BNP) were active in deprived areas, like where I went to university, and this exacerbated the "town and gown" divide. They perceived us in our ivory towers and we perceived them as the uneducated racists – racism was about marching and painting a St George's flag on the roof tiles, far removed from the post-racist world which I felt I inhabited. To acknowledge that my attainment was as much to do with my white male privilege as it was to do with my academic ability and effort would have been to distance myself from what I believed were my achievements. As an early career lecturer, I started to encounter students of colour but I perceived no difference between them and their peers, even buying into the myth that their over-representation in academic misconduct hearings was due to some cultural predilection for parroting as a form of respect. This is one area of decolonisation where I think we as an academic community still struggle: our view of education is that repetition of material is plagiarism and a form of cheating. I cannot even imagine how I would start a conversation in a HE institution that challenged this. Yet many of us have talked about how this is cultural, believing that in other countries education is different, that this repetition is not just okay but is taught and encouraged. Why have we accepted, without question, that the British HE perspective to this is the correct one and that other cultures have got it wrong? It was not until I was researching for my PhD that I realised my data showed that there was a disconnect between what I was observing in my students, which was constant micro-aggressions, and less often aggressions, and how students, both the oppressed and oppressors, described this bullying behaviour in interviews as confidence, preparedness and intelligence that it slowly started to dawn on me that our students of colour were being unfairly disadvantaged and that we were all ignoring it. Since then I have gone through stages of patronising those I had previously oppressed – another form of oppression – thinking that toolkits and checklists provided meaningful solutions, to my current position that can perhaps be best described as one of realising I am part of a problem but that I am unsure as to what the answer is.

How do we decolonise ourselves?

My ('Teleola's) perspective changed when I read the history of Black people in Britain, coupled with the historical narrative parroted in my country's history books that we, as Black people, were the problem – we were told, and believed, that but for the British and their "White Jesus", we'd still be savages living in huts. I had to re-educate myself to open my eyes to the reality of my own history. I had been through the same education system as most Afro-Caribbeans and had been taught about how the white man had first discovered and then civilised my homeland, as if it did not exist in a meaningful way until he noticed it.

The enlightenment was presented as the next stage of the development from the perceived savagery of my ancestors. Everything we had done and were doing was swept aside in order to be replaced by something that was seen to be the only way; to cling to our own traditions was backward and ignorant. We were supposed to be grateful for this gift of being civilised and in the most part we were. As critical race pedagogy (CRP) argues state-controlled education is popular because it is such an effective tool of emancipation – who is going to seek liberation if they are constantly told that they are not oppressed? I was raised as a Christian, told that I was created in the image of God. A God who when he took human form did not look like me, in fact the Church told us that the snow-white skin of Jesus and his mother were a sign of their purity. White Jesus offered salvation but only if we quietly accepted our positions and suffering in this life, ready to be rewarded in the next. One of the sources of my anger as I came to realise how colonised I had become was that this was a complete misrepresentation of the religious traditions on which these views claimed to be based: Jesus' whiteness is not biblical but an intentional construct of subsequent white institutions. White Jesus had been weaponised from the crusades onwards.

I started to learn what CRT calls anti-histories, grateful that the internet made material I was never given access to at school available to me. America seems both ahead of and behind the British in addressing race in HE; predominantly black colleges are world-leading in progressive action whilst many predominantly white institutions appear to be wilfully dragging their heels. This, coupled with the boon in popular literature written on identity, has meant that there has been an explosion in material available to someone who wishes to seek alternative narratives as I did. Historically, feminists have been feared by men and some women, because of the threat that equality might diminish the advantages men have enjoyed and the same is now true as the consciousness of people of colour is rising. In the same way that men became obsessed about what feminism said about them, labelling feminists as man-haters, many white people have looked at progressive movements like the #BlackLivesMatter movement and asked what it says about them. The reality is that the conversations are about women or people of colour respectively, they say nothing about white men, which may in itself create resentment from those used to being centre stage.

I got angry. Really angry. I could not talk to white people; I either avoided my partner, a white man, or actively sought an argument. How could all these white people be carrying on like nothing had happened whilst enjoying the benefits of enslaving my ancestors like animals? After a fortnight (and without physically harming my partner) I realised that I needed to channel this anger if it were to do anything other than harm me. Since then I have read, and read as much as I can, avidly consuming this new perspective. I have worked in HE on BAME focused projects, given conference papers, co-written this article, and taken every opportunity to generate positive change. The slow progress, and regular backward steps, reignite a visceral anger that I struggle to check. One example of the continual issues is the peer feedback we have received on this paper. Whilst I appreciate the constructive feedback from both reviewers which has greatly improved the article, one of the comments illustrated the conventions that have become accepted within HE as the right way to do things. We were asked to make our writing less emotive in places. I am, as explained above, emotive about this topic and question why I have to check that emotion before my voice can be heard. As a person of colour, I can contribute to sorting my side of things but there is a role for the other side, those who created and perpetuate this situation.

My (Nick's) journey of decolonisation has been a stumbling mess. I, like many white people, brought up to not mention colour, struggled to find the words to have the conversation. I now know that we need safe spaces perhaps as much as people of colour do in which we can ask what we should say and, most importantly, can listen. The academy is full of well-meaning people in positions of power convening meetings of various types to bring people together to discuss issues of race, only for white people to dominate the conversation and subject people of colour to the same micro-aggressions they are too used to. I was one of these people. I knew best. I was always passionate about pedagogy and I looked to learning and teaching for answers, still believing that I could ride in as a white saviour and make things better. I still struggle to listen. I am grateful to Joel Modiri for telling me in no uncertain terms that the Black community did not need whites to sit with them; if we wanted to be allies, we should work in our own communities. These are the communities that created and now perpetuate the status quo which is one of oppression. This feels harder than standing in solidarity though, but Joel is correct, there is plenty that I could remedy in my own community and to better effect. As a law academic I also still have difficulty empathising with 'Teleola's anger about historical harms; I am perhaps too used to stripping all of the emotion and the personal out of the stories behind the case law I teach and getting down to the core legal issues, the *ratio decidendi*. I wrote my MPhil thesis on the philosophical reasoning in the *Bland*[35] judgment. Anthony Bland had been crushed at the Hillsborough disaster. I was aware of the overly medicalised way in which the air being crushed out of him and his brain being deprived of oxygen was described in court. I had read the testimony that his Dad gave the court about seeing his son persist in a vegetative state. I was moved when reading how the hospital planned to sedate him as he died so his family would be saved from witnessing the contortions his body would otherwise go through. Yet, as my dual disciplines of law and philosophy had taught me, I mostly ignored the emotional and jumped to the rational, dissecting the logic of the arguments. I can teach about sexual violence, genocide and torture without getting upset and have seen this as a strength. I still sometimes find myself thinking that 'Teleola, also a law graduate, should surely be doing the same? I had also thought that historical distance would help with healing; after all slavery was abolished a long time ago. Yet there is no historical distance: Windrush, Grenfell and Covid-19 highlight how people of colour are still suffering today. I now talk about Grenfell in my teaching as an example of how the law of property serves some whilst forcing others to live in indescribable circumstances. I engage with the #BlackLivesMatter protests and frame the violence associated with some elements of that in the historical context of the violence done by the state against people of colour. I teach about the Prevent strategy as a racist policy. If I am honest though, these little acts of what feels like rebellion are ineffectual; if they make anyone feel better it is probably me. The entire epistemological framework of HE is institutionally discriminatory; it is not that it is not working but that it is working exactly as it should be. The discipline of law is also problematic: some of its greatest achievements in advancing equality and fairness still ignore that the whole universal framework of alleged right and wrong is a Eurocentric construction and another form of colonisation.

Why is self-decolonisation necessary to decolonise the curriculum?

Self-decolonisation is necessary because otherwise, we risk falling into the trap of colonising in a different guise, that of white saviours. From our experiences of delivering staff development sessions we have crudely categorised colleagues as the patronising liberal, the learning and teaching expert, or the colour-blind.

In his introduction to the 30th anniversary edition of *Pedagogy of the Oppressed* Donaldo Macedo talks of "facile liberals and pseudocritical educators"[36] with whom I (Nick), in my earlier career, belonged. The patronising liberal has the pretence of an understanding of the struggle of people of colour in a manner that can best be

[35] *Airedale NHS Trust v Bland* [1993] AC 789 (HL).
[36] Freire (n 11) 13.

described as sloganising. By flag waving with the anti-racist movement a feeling of understanding is gained that has the real risk of turning into paternalism. Freire is often misinterpreted as presenting a radical opinion on the methods of teaching rather than on the philosophical construct of the entire educational system. Those who perceive themselves as liberal, or even radical, therefore risk falling into the trap of becoming paternalistic. Whilst the effort to look after and do the best for our students should in no way be diminished the risk that this morphs into speaking for them is very real and the project of giving them a voice becomes the project of speaking for them. Hirsch in her writing characterises this as liberals having an expectation of gratitude for their supposed support.[37] I (Nick) have done this in my own teaching, auditing my reading lists to discover that the authors were predominantly pale, male and stale. Our first years studying English Legal System are now exposed to a diverse range of authors, which is certainly a good thing, but it exposes my naivety as I had honestly expected that the historical injustices of empire and slavery might be marched back by fiddling with what on the bookcase.

There is a further risk, characterised by the learning and teaching expert, that a solution based on teaching methodology can solve all ills. Active, as opposed to didactic, approaches to learning and teaching clearly present more opportunities for empowerment, but this has in some circles been misinterpreted into edicts for learning and teaching practice that seek change without realising the deep-seated nature of colonisation. That is in no way a defence of the status quo, which is in itself inadequate; rather it is a recognition that the problem runs deeper than teaching methodology. In our staff development work we have been asked for toolkits, take-aways, and sessions that can achieve the project of decolonisation in two hours. We have been told that staff will not do the reading but if we can give them a quick fix in a staff development workshop that would be great. In an industry which is based on exposure to thought and that has advanced some of the worst excesses of colonialism the request that the effort is made by people of colour to provide a simple solution for the majority is at best problematic. Toolkits and away-days are not going to solve the endemic problems of generations but the almost desperate desire for quick fixes in the OfS era has neither the will nor the capacity to recognise this. This is apparent in the lacklustre efforts to pay lip service to reducing progression, retention and attainment gaps when completing the self-audit for the Teaching Evaluation Framework (TEF). My ('Teleola's) last HE post was axed when the small amount of funding for work on these areas was withdrawn once the reports necessary for the TEF had been drafted. In seeing colonisation as only a learning and teaching issue there is also a distancing of it from the discipline-specific issues. When issues are placed in learning and teaching staff development sessions they often morph in the minds of academic staff into learning and teaching issues. At one staff development session a lecturer introduced himself and told 'Teleola he taught about the industrial revolution; when she asked how he taught his students about the influence of colonial Africans in driving this forward she was told that he was the subject expert and she was the learning and teaching expert. Suffice to say, the fact that without its empire Britain's industrial revolution would simply not be possible is still absent from the curriculum.

The colour-blind are a type of alleged anti-racist that exacerbates rather than diminishes the issues. It is primarily white people who claim not to see colour, refusing

[37] Hirsch (n 4) ch 4.

to acknowledge their own privilege and the oppression on which this is built. As race is an important aspect of the identity of many of us, refusing to see race is in reality the decision not to see people of colour. I ('Teleola) feel that when people claim not to see race, they are choosing not to see me as a black woman. This necessarily leads to not seeing the true issues and instead ascribing issues of race to other attributes. The belief is that Black people are doing as well as whites, and any differences in outcome are explained by merit, choices, or sometimes social class.[38] There are four beliefs that are ascribed to what is described as colour-blind racism.[39] The first is that society is meritocratic, the second that for most race is something they pay little or no attention to, the third that therefore any patterns of inequalities of outcomes for certain racial groups must be because of individual desert or collective cultural reasons, and the fourth that there is no therefore no need to act to address the causes of inequalities of outcome. This leads to a claim of objectivity and a belief that equality is about treating everyone in the same way without seeing that people start from very different places and that the enlightenment values that are claimed to be objective are in fact gendered and racialised in favour of white men. At my (Nick's) institution we are introducing, long overdue in my opinion, anonymous marking for coursework. This is in large part because student representatives keep telling us that students of colour believe that there may be partiality; whether or not they are right is not relevant here. My colleagues in the law subject group have taken great offence to this, they see it as an institutional attack on their integrity: how dare anyone imply that they are not professional enough to mark without bias? They are blind to race or gender, so their marking is beyond reproach. This demonstrates how deeply it is felt that not seeing colour is the right thing to do and how far we have to go to bring about change. Colour-blindness also leads to action that is targeted at a deficit as colour cannot be the cause of disadvantage, so workshops on resilience or study skills sessions are timetabled based on the belief that the solution is to remedy a problem within the student herself, requiring no change to the HE institution or the staff within it.

Conclusion

We are in a situation where the power to change things for the better rests with white power-holders and the ability to action that change rests with the oppressed. The space for action therefore must necessarily be at the intersection of these two groups – unless power is going to be taken by force. The real and present danger is that this is the same space in which previous action has occurred, where white power-holders have, under the guise of reducing inequalities, in fact been self-serving, which, as noted above, Bell describes as "interest convergence". White power-holders cannot work from within Black communities, this would itself be a form of colonisation. White people have plenty of problems within their own communities which they could usefully work to address, and this is where their solidarity is best expressed. Ultimately the role of white people must be to work within their own communities to create the circumstances in which white power-holders relinquish at least some of their power to those they have oppressed, unconditionally and with the full realisation that this will damage their own short-term interests. This power needs to come with the resource to enact far-reaching

[38]Forman (n 3).
[39]ibid.

root and branch change. If people of colour are not given the power to remedy historic injustices and continuing oppression then the only realistic option is an insurgent pedagogy in which they take the power for themselves and if this happens those who are white and decolonised can do little more stand aside and wish them luck.

Disclosure statement

No potential conflict of interest was reported by the authors.

Decolonising the master's house: how Black Feminist epistemologies can be and are used in decolonial strategy

Oluwaseun Matiluko

ABSTRACT
Understanding Black Feminist thinking and decolonial strategy as intimately connected, this paper argues that the foregrounding of Black Feminist epistemology is crucial in the decolonisation of university curricula. Focusing specifically on British undergraduate law curricula this paper argues that Black British Feminist modes of thought could produce effective and long-lasting change in the way that we teach and learn about law, that could bring an end to colonial continuities. The first two sections of this paper explain what exactly is meant by "decolonisation", "Black Feminist epistemology" and "Black British Feminism", while the last two sections look at how a Black British Feminist decolonisation of legal curricula could take place.

Introduction

Audre Lorde, later known as Gamba Adisa, famously wrote an essay entitled *The Master's Tools Will Never Dismantle the Master's House.*[1] Within the short essay, she described an issue which she saw within feminism of the late twentieth century, in that white feminists were continuing to utilise the tools of "racist patriarchy".[2] From her perspective, America was a "racist patriarchy", a country built on settler-colonialism, where white men were privileged off the backs of native groups, enslaved Africans and subjugated women.[3] Lorde, and her radical 1970s black feminist contemporaries within the Combahee River Collective, believed that if America continued to subordinate any groups in order to privilege others then America would never truly be the "land of the free".[4]

Thus, in her essay on the master's tools, Lorde warned the white women who were leading the charge in the mainstream American feminist movement not to continue to uphold oppression whilst fighting for women's liberation. She argued that feminism must not just be about middle-class white women but include all women. Therefore,

---

[1]Audre Lorde, *Sister Outsider* (Crossing Press 2007) 110.
[2]ibid.
[3]ibid.
[4]Combahee River Collective, "The Combahee River Collective Statement" in Keeanga-Yamahtta Taylor (ed), *How We Get Free: Black Feminism and the Combahee River Collective* (Haymarket Books 2012) 19; Lorde (n 1) 22–23.

the mainstream feminist movement should seek to acknowledge more marginalised women and learn more about their differences and connections.[5] Lorde argued that, by understanding each other's differences, feminism could be for every woman and become a truly inclusive and effective fight against oppression.[6] Women would never have a shot at dismantling the master's house by using the master's tools.

Professor Kehinde Andrews, the first UK-based Black Studies professor, uses Lorde's metaphor in his writing about decolonisation and the university, describing the university as the master's house.[7] He suggests that the university can never truly be decolonised as it continues to "retain its role in creating the knowledge that reproduces a vastly unequal status quo".[8] For example, the racial types and stereotypes that are now pervasive public knowledge were first developed in European universities, which enabled the horrors of the transatlantic slave trade and late-modern colonialism.[9]

Andrews offers recolonisation as a solution, arguing that true decolonisation of the master's house/university is impossible.[10] However, in this paper I argue that the university can be decolonised, because if Black Feminist thought is foregrounded in decolonial strategy, university curricula *can* be decolonised. If we cease from using the master's tools, the master's house will fall and open spaces for new modes of thought.

Nevertheless, often academic arguments that discuss concepts such as "decolonisation" and "Black Feminism" can become quite intractable, as scholars fail to define exactly what they mean. Therefore, in the first two sections of this paper, I will define what I mean by decolonisation, Black Feminism and Black British Feminism within the university context. In the final two sections I will then explain what Black British Feminist decolonisation of university curricula could look like, focusing on legal curricula and using as a case study a European university where an attempt at Black Feminist decolonisation has been carried out.

What is decolonisation?

A layperson would likely describe decolonisation as the instance of a foreign power granting sovereignty to a former colony. In other words, what Michael Collins calls "formal flag independence", or "the achievement of sovereign nation-statehood by a previously colonised territory".[11] Decolonisation can also be used to describe the process whereby land is returned to indigenous inhabitants. And it has also been used to describe the process of granting citizenship to former colonial subjects. In the French Caribbean, for example, moving from a colony to a *département d'outre-mer* in 1946 was seen by many of the inhabitants of Martinique, French Guiana and Guadeloupe as a form of decolonial liberation.[12]

[5] Lorde (n 1) 112–13.
[6] ibid.
[7] Kehinde Andrews, "The Challenge for Black Studies in the Neoliberal University" in Gurminder K Bhambra, Kerem Nisancioglu and Dalia Gebrial (eds), *Decolonising the University* (Pluto Press 2018) 138.
[8] ibid 139.
[9] Marius Turda and Maria Sophia Quine, *Historicizing Race* (Bloomsbury Publishing 2018).
[10] Andrews (n 7) 139.
[11] Michael Collins, "Decolonization" in John M MacKenzie (ed), *The Encyclopaedia of Empire* (1st edn, John Wiley & Sons 2016) 1.
[12] Annette K Joseph-Gabriel, "Gerty Archimède and the Struggle for Decolonial Citizenship in the French Antilles, 1946-51" in Félix Germain and Silyane Larcher (eds), *Black French Women and the Struggle for Equality, 1848-2016* (University of Nebraska Press 2018).

Indeed, scholars like Eve Tuck and K. Wayne Yang contend that decolonisation can encapsulate only material reality, like in the above examples, and not an abstract or "metaphorical" one.[13] However across the world, decolonisation is a term that has taken on a new life of its own with many focusing not only on the struggle for land and land rights, but also on how structures can be decolonised, with the university often taking centre-stage in these discussions.[14] This is something that initially started in formerly colonised countries, like Kenya, and is now being discussed in former colonial metropoles – it is not only the colonised who must undergo decolonisation.[15]

Activists and scholars argue that European (particularly) imperial colonial ideas and structures continue to permeate academic institutions. This is because major European Empires ended relatively recently in the late twentieth century, and thus it is argued that we are still dealing with the material consequences of those empires – we are still very much living in the aftershocks of European conquest. For example, looking empirically, many now-independent nations in Africa are European colonial constructs – as are those in the Americas, in Oceania and Asia. The global reach of languages like English, Spanish and French came about because of Empire. In Europe in particular, one can see how multiculturalism has arisen due to Empire: most black Britons and black Frenchmen are direct descendants of former British/French Caribbean/African colonial subjects.[16]

Moreover, much of our present understanding of "race" is linked to the race science developed by universities in these European Empires, from grouping of peoples into categories of "white" and "black", to ideas and stereotypes imposed upon these categories that are still pervasive to this day.[17] For example, the idea that black people have "super strength" was a crucial rationale behind European trafficking of enslaved Africans, an instrumental ideology in the crafting of colonial policy in Africa (most notably in Charles Mangin's conception of the *Force Noire*), and continues to influence use of state force against black groups in some parts of the Western world.[18]

Therefore, seeing that much of the world we live in has been epistemologically constructed by European Empires that have disenfranchised racialised groups, scholars and activists argue that their colonial ideas continue to influence the world – and the university. In universities it is submitted that these colonial continuities, or "coloniality",

---

[13]Eve Tuck and K Wayne Yang, "Decolonization Is Not a Metaphor" (2012) 1 Decolonization: Indigeneity, Education & Society 1.

[14]Wanelisa Xaba, "Challenging Fanon: A Black Radical Feminist Perspective on Violence and the Fees Must Fall Movement" (2017) 31(3–4) Agenda 96, 98; Nelson Maldonado-Torres, "Outline of Ten Theses on Coloniality and Decoloniality" (*Caribbean Studies Association*) <http://caribbeanstudiesassociation.org/docs/Maldonado-Torres_Outline_Ten_Theses-10.23.16.pdf> accessed 4 September 2019.

[15]For example, Ngugi wa Thiong'o is well known for his work in decolonising literature in sub-Saharan Africa as discussed in *Decolonising the Mind: The Politics of Language in African Literature* (James Currey 2009).

[16]Anthony F Heath and others (eds), *The Political Integration of Ethnic Minorities in Britain* (Oxford University Press 2013) 19–26; "Census Analysis: Ethnicity and Religion of the Non-UK Born Population in England and Wales: 2011" (*Office for National Statistics*) <www.ons.gov.uk/peoplepopulationandcommunity/culturalidentity/ethnicity/articles/2011censusanalysisethnicityandreligionofthenonukbornpopulationinenglandandwales/2015-06-18> accessed 10 May 2020; Dominic Thomas, *Black France: Colonialism, Immigration, and Transnationalism* (Indiana University Press 2007).

[17]Turda and Quine (n 9).

[18]Sujit Sivasundaram, "Race, Empire, and Biology before Darwinism" in Denis R Alexander and Ronald L Numbers (eds), *Biology and Ideology from Descartes to Dawkins* (University of Chicago Press 2010) 120–24; Crawford Young, *The African Colonial State in Comparative Perspective* (Yale University Press 1994) 106; Simon Pemberton, "Demystifying Deaths in Police Custody: Challenging State Talk" (2008) 17 Social & Legal Studies 237, 249.

exist in the ways in which courses are taught. Western epistemologies are taught as core substantive material whilst epistemologies from marginalised groups are taught as an externalised "other" or are excluded from a narrative of which they are a central part.[19] The imperial worldview is the cake, while Third World epistemologies are sprinkles sparingly added on at the end.

This particularisation of the universal, in other words, the tendency to present racialised communities as the "other", can go unnoticed because within the university knowledge is often presented as neutral: as Achille Mbembe argues there is a supposed "detachment of the known from the knower".[20] And this can be seen within British legal curricula.

To obtain a qualifying law degree in England and Wales one must study a number of foundational subjects: equity and trusts, land law, European Union law, public law, criminal law and law of obligations.[21] Most universities offer optional subjects including employment law, intellectual property law, jurisprudence, Roman law and legal history.[22] However, despite the fact that the British Empire only formally ended in 1997 and that law was a key conduit through which Empire was enacted, ideas, histories and scholarship of peoples from outside the Western hegemonic norm are rarely interrogated in our legal curricula.[23] To adopt the phraseology of Lewis Gordon, non-hegemonic or "problem people are [often] derailed from the dialectics of recognition".[24]

Nevertheless, if one were to interrogate our legal curricula, and analyse the histories of the norms, ratios and obiters that we routinely impress upon students, Empire can often be found bubbling beneath the surface. For instance, in jurisprudence students are often taught about different theories of law and how the law can and should relate to society. Thus, students are required to engage with the writings of figures like John Stuart Mill, Jeremy Bentham and John Locke. However, what is often neglected in teaching these works is that many of these scholars grew up, studied, practised and taught within the lifespan of Empire. Therefore, instead of presenting their theories as though they are detached "from the knower", it would be useful to illustrate how, far

---

[19] Nelson Maldonado-Torres, "On the Coloniality of Being: Contributions to the Development of a Concept" (2007) 21 Cultural Studies 240, 243–51; Seun Matiluko, "Where Are the Black Scientists, Artists and Thinkers in University Syllabuses?" *The Guardian* (London, 18 July 2018) <www.theguardian.com/higher-education-network/2018/jul/18/where-are-the-black-scientists-artists-and-thinkers-in-university-syllabuses> accessed 2 May 2020; Decolonising SOAS Working Group, "Decolonising SOAS: Learning and Teaching Toolkit for Programme and Module Convenors" (May 2018) 8 <https://blogs.soas.ac.uk/decolonisingsoas/files/2018/10/Decolonising-SOAS-Learning-and-Teaching-Toolkit-AB.pdf> accessed 6 September 2019.

[20] Walter Mignolo, *Local Histories/Global Designs: Coloniality, Subaltern Knowledges, and Border Thinking* (Princeton University Press 2000) 67; Achille Mbembe, "Decolonizing Knowledge and the Question of the Archive" (*Africa Is a Country*, 2015) <https://africaisacountry.atavist.com/decolonizing-knowledge-and-the-question-of-the-archive> accessed 4 September 2019.

[21] The Law Society, "Qualifying with a Law Degree" (*Law Society*, 28 August 2019) <www.lawsociety.org.uk/law-careers/becoming-a-solicitor/qualifying-with-a-degree/qualifying-with-a-law-degree/> accessed 6 September 2019.

[22] For example, "Programme Structure: Honours Law (LLB) – What's Running in 2020/21" (*University of Bristol*) <www.bris.ac.uk/unit-programme-catalogue/RouteStructure.jsa?_ga=2.11119602.754879191.1540287707-1257199379.1525950554&ayrCode=20%2F21&byCohort=N&programmeCode=9LAWD001U> accessed 10 May 2020; "Options and Core Courses" (*University of Oxford*) <www.law.ox.ac.uk/admissions/options?year=All&programme=7907> accessed 20 May 2020; "Course Detail" (*King's College London*) <www.kcl.ac.uk/study/undergraduate/courses/law-llb> accessed 20 May 2020.

[23] Young (n 18) 79–91; Lauren Benton and Lisa Ford, *Rage for Order: The British Empire and the Origins of International Law, 1800-1850* (Harvard University Press 2016) 78–81; Antony Anghie, *Imperialism, Sovereignty and the Making of International Law* (Cambridge University Press 2007) 13–58.

[24] Lewis R Gordon, "Disciplinary Decadence and the Decolonisation of Knowledge" (2014) 39(1) Africa Development 81, 88.

from being purely theoretical, John Austin's "command theory" of law was a reality for many under British imperial rule.[25] Austin was a prominent British jurist, who headed up four commissions into imperial Malta, and did not envisage British rule in the colonies as being indirect, as it would later become in much of sub-Saharan Africa, but rather believed in directly ruling the colonies with total disregard for indigenous customs.[26] In fact, this form of legal positivism, per Antony Anghie and Karuna Mantena's analysis, encapsulated much of early nineteenth-century imperial rule in the British Empire.[27]

Similarly, it would be useful to understand how Locke believed that, while all are "born free", children are born "not yet able to practice liberty", and thus could be governed without their consent until reaching adulthood.[28] Seeing the non-white people that Britain conquered as perennial children, Locke extended this belief further, suggesting that while all human beings were equal some were more equal than others and thus could rule over them without their consent.[29] And it would be useful to understand how John Stuart Mill regarded international law as applying not to "barbarous peoples", but only to civilised ones.[30] In fact, he considered that granting subject races sovereignty would be "a certain evil" due to their intellectual inferiority.[31] Understanding that jurisprudence is not merely theory but has often been theory *and* practice could, perhaps, aid decolonisation of legal curricula, as it would enable discussion on how law and the science of law have shaped not only British society but that of the wider world.

This, however, is not just an issue for jurisprudence within legal curricula. For example, equity and trusts teaching could acknowledge the pervasive colonial history embedded within trusts law, instead of treating seminal cases like *Saunders v Vautier*, a case concerning stock in the East India Company, as politically neutral cases from which one only has to learn the ratio.[32] Furthermore, land law lecturers could discuss how ideas of private property came to be developed in the first place, highlighting how the British doctrine of *terra nullius* shaped conquest in North America, New Zealand and Australia in different ways, sometimes resulting in recognition of aboriginal property rights and sometimes not.[33]

I point out all of this to say that we need a wider understanding of our laws and what they have been used for in the past if, in the present, we truly want a generation of enlightened lawyers. It would be impossible to teach everything about everything, but the fact remains that imperial history permeates the entirety of our law. Understanding the history of how certain legal doctrines and ideas have developed will, as is often the case with history, enable us to learn from the mistakes of the past and to develop better ideas for the future instead of perpetuating more of the same.

---

[25] Mbembe (n 20); Raymond Wacks, *Understanding Jurisprudence: An Introduction to Legal Theory* (5th edn, Oxford University Press 2017) 80–91.

[26] Benton and Ford (n 23) 7 and 114–15.

[27] Anghie (n 23) 32–115; Karuna Mantena, *Alibis of Empire* (Princeton University Press 2010) 7–9.

[28] Uday Mehta, *Liberalism and Empire: A Study in Nineteenth-Century British Liberal Thought* (University of Chicago Press 1999) 61.

[29] ibid 61–78.

[30] Peter Fitzpatrick, "Terminal Legality" in Diane Kirkby and Catharine Coleborne (eds), *Law, History, Colonialism: The Reach of Empire* (Manchester University Press 2009) 17.

[31] Mantena (n 27) 36.

[32] [1841] EWHC Ch J82, (1841) 4 Beav 115 8.

[33] Stuart Banner, "Why *Terra Nullius*? Anthropology and Property Law in Early Australia" (2005) 23 (1) Law and History Review 95, 111–31.

This would be disrupting "coloniality" – by painting a wider picture when we teach students, we create a classroom open to epistemic diversity.[34] Therefore, decolonisation can never be what some in the reactionary press claim it to be; it is not scrapping Mozart for Stormzy nor "dethroning some of the greatest ... thinkers in western culture simply because they were white men".[35] Decolonisation is not about segregation or annexation but rather is about conversation between knowledges. Thus, for example, "diversity" by way of adding some brown faces into the curriculum, but not changing how the curriculum is taught, can never be true decolonisation.[36]

Understanding decolonisation in this sense draws direct parallels to the concepts underpinning Black Feminism. Black Feminism challenges the notion of there being one way to exist as a woman, thereby unmasking the dominant narrative as just one of many available narratives. Therefore, just as the objective behind decolonisation is to open up the way we receive knowledge and avoid perpetuating colonial narratives that continue to "other" those we consider to be non-hegemonic voices, so it is with Black Feminism.

Black Feminism

Most who refer to "Black Feminism" typically mean "African-American feminism". Many pinpoint one of the earliest instances of the development of African-American feminist thought to a speech made by Sojourner Truth in 1851. While the exact wording of her speech is contested, she made a speech in front of a group of predominantly white women, arguing candidly that black women deserved rights too. This was within an era of women's suffrage where white women, like Susan B. Antony, would openly declare: "I will cut off this right arm of mine before I will ever work or demand the ballot for the Negro and not the woman."[37] Thus, Truth's speech questioned the then predominant essentialist narrative of what it was to be a female in America, pointing out that those who are both "negro" and "woman" deserve rights too.[38]

As Barbara Smith, founding member of the Combahee River Collective, has declared, this "concept of the simultaneity of oppression is ... the crux of a Black Feminist understanding of political reality", and that is perhaps most famously illustrated today through Kimberlé Crenshaw's conception of "intersectionality".[39] Intersectionality, which is now held in great esteem amongst many feminists, emanates from Crenshaw's work within the academic discipline known as critical race theory (CRT). CRT was birthed from critical legal scholarship (CLS), which emerged from 1970s

---

[34]Mbembe (n 20).

[35]Gabriella Swerling, "Stormzy Should Be Taught in Schools instead of Mozart to Prevent Exclusions, Charity Urges" *Telegraph* (London, 22 May 2019) <www.telegraph.co.uk/news/2019/05/21/stormzy-should-taught-schools-instead-mozart-prevent-exclusions/ 6 September 2019; Melanie Phillips, "Decolonising Curriculums Is Sinister and Wrong" *The Times* (London, 19 February 2019) <www.thetimes.co.uk/article/decolonising-curriculums-is-sinister-and-wrong-0vc5s2dm0> accessed 16 September 2019.

[36]Nathaniel Coleman, "Diversity Is a Dirty Word" (*Academia*, 2015).

[37]Angela Davis, *Women, Race & Class* (Vintage Books 1983) 118.

[38]Kimberlé Crenshaw, "Demarginalizing the Intersection of Race and Sex: A Black Feminist Critique of Antidiscrimination Doctrine, Feminist Theory and Antiracist Politics" [1989] University of Chicago Legal Forum 139, 153.

[39]Patricia Hill Collins, "What's in a Name? Womanism, Black Feminism, and Beyond" (1996) 26(1) The Black Scholar 9, 13; Barbara Smith, "Introduction" in Barbara Smith (ed), *Home Girls: A Black Feminist Anthology* (Rutgers University Press 2000) xxxiv.

American academia although it is most often associated with Harvard University, where Crenshaw herself obtained her JD.[40]

As Harvard academic Roberto Unger describes it, the CLS movement stemmed from a "leftist tradition in modern legal thought and practice".[41] The scholars involved, and who continue to develop CLS, believe(d) that law is not innately moral or objective or commonsensical but rather, a value-ridden construction that can in turn be deconstructed.[42] CRT is an offshoot of this movement with distinct dissimilarities from it, for example most CRT scholars embrace the idea of individual rights while many CLS scholars reject them.[43] Difference underpins CRT, or rather what Angela Harris calls the "politics of difference", in which supposedly neutral legal structures are deconstructed with the racial disparities they produce laid bare.[44]

Therefore, Crenshaw's conception of intersectionality has its roots in CRT but is explicitly linked to Black Feminism. Just as those in the Combahee River Collective believe that black women experience simultaneous "interlocking oppression(s)", which make their lived experiences different from those of black men and white women, Crenshaw argues that black women face different obstacles from those faced by white women and black men and that this "intersection of oppression" is exposed in a racialised justice system.[45] In Crenshaw's conception of intersectionality, discrimination is described as though the person being discriminated against is standing at the centre of an intersection,[46] and can be hit by traffic coming from different directions. Therefore, as the analogy goes, if a black woman is discriminated against, they may be hit by traffic symbolising any one of gender, race, sexuality, all three or more. Thus, any number of combinations of traffic coming from any number of oppressions can meet in the middle to harm this woman.[47] This is what Sojourner Truth was alluding to in 1851 when she suggested that the experiences of black women in America are different from those of white women. This is what 1970s feminist Angela Davis was writing about when she said that "we cannot … look at gender in isolation from race [and] from class".[48] And this is what twenty-first-century Black Feminists, like those who founded the Black Lives Matter movement, write about when they argue that black women are oppressed due to both their race and their gender identity.[49]

However, Black Feminist epistemology is not just limited to understandings of "interlocking oppression". Indeed, as Crenshaw herself notes, intersectionality is not a "grand theory of everything", but rather a tool that helps to describe problems rather than solve them.[50] Therefore, exploring Black Feminist scholarship further, it is apparent that, aside from its core tenet of non-essentialism, many Black Feminists consider

[40]Adrien Katherine Wing, "Critical Race Feminism: Legal Reform for the Twenty-first Century" in John Solomos and David Theo Goldberg (eds), *A Companion to Racial and Ethnic Studies* (Blackwell 2002) 160–67.
[41]Roberto Mangabeira Unger, *The Critical Legal Studies Movement* (Harvard University Press 1986) 1.
[42]ibid 5–15.
[43]Kimberlé Crenshaw, "Race, Reform, and Retrenchment: Transformation and Legitimation in Antidiscrimination Law" (1988) 101(7) Harvard Law Review 1331, 1357–58.
[44]Angela P Harris, "The Jurisprudence of Reconstruction" (1994) 82 California Law Review 741, 744.
[45]Keeanga-Yamahtta Taylor, "Introduction" in Taylor (n 4) 4–20.
[46]Crenshaw, "Demarginalizing the Intersection of Race and Sex" (n 38) 149.
[47]ibid.
[48]Angela Davis, *Freedom Is a Constant Struggle: Ferguson, Palestine, and the Foundations of a Movement* (Haymarket Books 2016) 41.
[49]Black Lives Matter, "Herstory" https://blacklivesmatter.com/herstory/ accessed 6 September 2019.
[50]Kimberlé Crenshaw, "Postscript" in Helma Lutz, Maria Teresa Herrera Vivar and Linda Supik (eds), *Framing Intersectionality: Debates on a Multi-Faceted Concept in Gender Studies* (Routledge 2016) 232; Joanne Conaghan, "Intersectionality and the Feminist Project in Law" in Emily Grabham and others (eds), *Intersectionality and Beyond: Law, Power and the Politics of Location* (Routledge 2009) 8.

historical understandings of the present to be crucial to their epistemologies. For instance, many Black Feminist scholars and activists have written and spoken about the racial history of the Americas and how black people's first mass encounter with the Americas was through the prism of slavery (with black women specifically oppressed as slave producers), therefore, black women have ended up at the bottom of a racial hierarchy in a white dominant and heterosexist nation.[51] In this sense, due to the importance of non-essentialism and subaltern historiographies to Black Feminism, it can be regarded as a decolonial mode of thought in that it seeks to uncover and understand the experiences of the "other" instead of perpetuating a Eurocentric norm.

It is important to note, however, that it is not only African-American women who have been articulating Black Feminism. In actuality, black women globally have long been articulating Black Feminist ideals, just within different contexts.[52] Black British Feminism emerged in the twentieth century, after large swathes of black migration to the UK, and was developed in an explicitly anti-colonial context – linking the present experience of black British womanhood to the global histories of the British Empire within which their foremothers were oppressed.[53] Black people in Britain today are descendants of subjects of the British Empire. The British Empire was extensively involved in the transatlantic slave trade – they brought the first enslaved Africans to the Americas in 1619. Then, in the wake of abolitionism in the 1800s, the Empire commenced colonisation of various parts of Africa based on the rationale that blacks, while no longer regarded as chattel, were innately inferior to whites and needed exposure to superior European civilisation in order to develop.[54] In the twentieth century, in both the colonial and postcolonial era, many black people migrated to the metropole, provoking Ambalavaner Sivanandan's aphorism, "we are here because you were there".[55]

Therefore, Black British feminists typically reference black British women's experiences as different from those of white women and of black men, but root this explicitly in histories of Empire. This is in contrast to African-American feminists who root their epistemologies within the context of North American conquest. Thus, Claudia Jones – a British subject who grew up in America and then was later deported to the United Kingdom – articulated the idea of "triple oppression" in the 1940s.[56] Arguing that the "Negro woman [was] the most exploited and oppressed", she made the case that the oppression of black women was distinct from that of black men and white women due to black women's oppression being based on their subordinate gender, race and class.[57] This was explicitly rooted in an anti-colonial perspective, with Jones writing that: "imperialism [is] the root cause of racialism. It is the ideology which upholds ... exploitation".[58]

[51]Hill Collins (n 39) 4; bell hooks, *Yearning* (Routledge 2015) 57; Charles Mills, "Intersecting Contracts" in Carole Pateman and Charles Mills (eds), *Contract & Domination* (Polity Press 2007) 173.

[52]Akwugo Emejulu and Francesca Sobande, "Introduction: On the Problems and Possibilities of European Black Feminism and Afrofeminism" in Akwugo Emejulu and Francesca Sobande (eds), *To Exist Is to Resist: Black Feminism in Europe* (Pluto Press 2019) 5–6.

[53]Beverley Bryan, Stella Dadzie and Suzanne Scafe, *The Heart of the Race: Black Women's Lives in Britain* (Verso 2018) 1–16.

[54]Turda and Quine (n 9) 73–94.

[55]Cited in Avery F Gordon, "On 'Lived Theory': An Interview with A. Sivanandan" (2014) 55(4) Race & Class 1, 2.

[56]Carole Boyce Davies, *Left of Karl Marx: The Political Life of Black Communist Claudia Jones* (Duke University Press 2008) 143 by National Women's Commission, Communist Party USA.

[57]Claudia Jones, "An End to the Neglect of the Problems of the Negro Woman!" (reprinted from Political Affairs June 1949) 18.

[58]As cited in Davies (n 56) 87.

Similarly, other prominent Black British feminists of the twentieth century, such as the Organisation of Women of African and Asian Descent (OWAAD), felt the same. They agreed that Jones' thesis of "triple oppression" was "the bedrock of it all" – showing that Black British Feminism is self-reproducing and does not just borrow from American modes of thought.[59] They wrote explicitly in their black feminist constitution that "because of [their] historical experiences under Colonialism and slavery" they recognised that it is "imperialism" that has utilised: "racism to justify their rape of our countries and our people ... we do not regard our liberation as Black women as a possibility, unless it is part of the world-wide struggle against Imperialism".[60]

Indeed, Black British feminists, as opposed to the vast majority of African-American feminists, regularly explicitly tie their experiences and their politics to black communities abroad. Black British Feminism is also distinguishable due to the vestiges of "political blackness" within it. When OWAAD first formed in February 1978, it was the Organisation of Women of Africa and African Descent, a group for women who either had "their origins in Africa or who ... now have their immediate origins in ... [the] Caribbean".[61] However by August 1978 OWAAD had transformed to include South Asian women, realising their shared connections as formerly colonised subjects within the imperial metropole.[62] This was part of a wider trend in Britain which has come to be known as "political blackness", in which some activist groups, comprised predominantly of non-white members, band together under the banner of blackness.[63] This perhaps reflects what Gayatri Spivak calls "strategic essentialism" – when you are in a minority group it can be a better political tactic to combine with other minority groups rather than to go it alone.[64]

Nevertheless, political blackness is no longer a popular framework. While there is still strong solidarity between those of black African descent and those of South Asian descent, they no longer combine under the banner of blackness as that can often obfuscate their distinct issues. Indeed, this is in part why many black British people dislike the new homogenising term of the twenty-first century – BAME (Black Asian and Minority Ethnic).[65] And this is in part why OWAAD folded in 1982.[66] Although some organisations continue to represent all non-white peoples whilst calling themselves "black", most black British groups today operate on an understanding that, while they have solidarity with other racialised groups around the world and in Britain, a person can only call themselves black if they are a member of the black African diaspora.[67]

Conclusively, the hallmarks of Black British Feminism are transnational solidarity, imperialism is the root of oppression, and that black women face oppression due to multiple factors, particularly, their race, their gender and their class. This indicates a strong connection between Black British Feminist epistemologies and decolonial

---

[59] Bryan and others (n 53).
[60] OWAAD Draft Constitution p 3, Black Cultural Archives DADZIE 1/1.
[61] ibid.
[62] Bryan and others (n 53) 164–65.
[63] Lola Young, "What Is Black British Feminism?" (2000) 11 Women: A Cultural Review 45, 55.
[64] Gayatri Chakravorty Spivak, "Subaltern Studies: Deconstructing Historiography" in D Landry and G MacLean (eds), *The Spivak Reader* (Routledge 1996) 214.
[65] Nadine White, "'As If the "B" in BAME Is Silent': Are Javid and Patel a Victory for All Ethnic Minorities?" (*Huffington Post*, 27 July 2019) <www.huffingtonpost.co.uk/entry/javid-and-patel-face-bame-community-backlash_uk_5d39d188e4b0419fd339692e> accessed 20 June 2020.
[66] Bryan and others (n 53) 257–60.
[67] "BSC Name Change Consultation: The Results Are In" (*NUS Connect*, 6 March 2018) <www.nusconnect.org.uk/articles/bsc-name-change-consultation-the-results-are-in> accessed 17 September 2019.

epistemologies, as both are explicitly rooted in critique of Empire, transnational, wanting to subvert colonial structures and prioritise presenting pluriversal viewpoints rather than supposedly universal ones. Therefore, this suggests that a praxis which foregrounds Black British Feminist epistemologies would be very effective in the decolonisation of British university curricula.

Black Feminist decolonisation in practice

However, while decolonisation of the university is something that is increasingly being pushed, there are many who have ignored the utility of Black Feminism within their activism or have acknowledged it in name but not in spirit.[68] This has caused issues within prominent university decolonisation movements. For example, in the South African #RhodesMustFall,[69] (RMF) and closely linked #Fees Must Fall (FMF), movements, intersectionality was acknowledged by many in those movements as one of their three key pillars.[70] Yet, intersectionality fails when it is utilised as a buzzword and not as praxis.[71] In South Africa many of the most marginalised students felt excised from and ignored by the wider movement, feeling that instead of practising intersectionality, many of the leaders of the movement were instead trying to deploy a pseudo-decolonisation that Fanon described, replacing one "species of men" with another one.[72] Thus, the RMF and FMF decolonisation movements in South Africa have become increasingly fractured.[73]

This is why, within the university space, it is not enough to simply declare that one is undertaking Black Feminist decolonisation, it must be overt in praxis. Although relatively few scholars have discussed decolonising university curricula from the perspective of Black *British* Feminism, some prominent scholars have posited frameworks for how Black Feminist epistemologies may be incorporated in the decolonisation of the university.[74] For instance, Ronaldo Vázquez and Rosalba Icaza have written about their work in decolonising the curricula at the University of Amsterdam, one of the oldest institutions in Europe.[75] In 2015, a diverse group of students occupied the University of Amsterdam, demanding decolonisation and were able to set the groundwork for change there.[76] A Diversity Commission was established which, despite its name, was concerned not just with replacing white faces with brown faces but with investigating what knowledge was being produced and how it was taught.[77] Using an intersectional decolonial praxis, Vázquez and Icaza detailed a framework which would help effectively

---

68 Bhambra and others (n 7) 1.

69 Francesca Sobande, "Black Feminist Contributions to Decolonizing the Curriculum" in Julie Cupples and Ramón Grosfoguel (eds), *Unsettling Eurocentrism in the Westernized University* (Routledge 2018) 89.

70 Xaba (n 14) 99; Abdul Kayum Ahmed, "The Rise of Fallism: #RhodesMustFall and the Movement to Decolonize the University" (PhD thesis, Columbia University 2019) 2.

71 Kathy Davis, "Intersectionality as Buzzword: A Sociology of Science Perspective on What Makes Feminist Theory Successful" in Lutz and others (n 50).

72 Xaba (n 14) 101–02; Frantz Fanon, *The Wretched of the Earth* (Constance Farrington tr, Penguin Books 2001) 27.

73 Ahmed (n 70) 206.

74 Olivia U Rutazibwa, "On Babies and Bathwater: Decolonizing International Development Studies" in Sara de Jong, Rosalba Icaza and Olivia U Rutazibwa (eds), *Decolonization and Feminisms in Global Teaching and Learning* (Routledge 2019) 168.

75 Rosalba Icaza and Ronaldo Vázquez, "Diversity of Decolonisation? Researching Diversity at the University of Amsterdam" in Bhambra and others (n 7) 113.

76 ibid 112.

77 ibid 114.

decolonise the university, and persuasively concluded that pedagogies of *positionality*, *relationality* and *transition* were paramount to an intersectional decolonisation of the university.[78]

Positionality in their framework means the recognition of origins of knowledge, so instead of presenting knowledge as an unquestionable hegemonic norm, a decolonised curriculum should address exactly where knowledge is coming from and the power dynamics underlying its production.[79] This is both decolonial and Black feminist, in that it interrogates the geopolitical context from which information arises and unveils who exactly is creating knowledge and why certain people's knowledges are valued over others due to their intersectional identities.[80] Or to paraphrase Rutazibwa, their understanding of positionality critiques who has a seat at the table and who does not.[81]

Per their framework, relationality means that teachers should acknowledge each individual's intersectional identity formation in their teaching, and reflect on how that may affect how they relate to taught subject-matter,[82] essentially questioning why some students relate more to some pieces of knowledge and not others. This is both decolonial and Black feminist as the teacher acknowledges the social hierarchies present in society, and ensures that the most marginalised students feel that they have room to speak instead of letting racial-gender politics play out in the classroom where the most privileged dominate conversation.[83] As the Combahee River Collective argues, when the most marginalised voices are engaged, we are able to ensure liberation for all, and not just the privileged few.[84] Finding ways for students to relate the curriculum to their own life experience not only allows for a more engaging classroom experience but also allows for discussion to widen instead of falling into a hegemonic universal narrative.[85]

Finally, regarding transitionality, Vázquez and Icaza question the purpose of the production of knowledge.[86] They look at knowledge production as often being a source of oppression: after all, it was in the university that the ideas of racial hierarchy that still exist today were first propagated.[87] Recognising how the university is "implicated in the politics of knowledge", this part of the Black Feminist decolonial framework dispels the myth that the university is a place where noble, politically neutral, people go to discover more about the world.[88] Instead, it recognises the reality that the university is often a space that produces and reproduces negative social realities.[89] Transitionality, in essence, is about questioning whether or not one is continuing to appropriate the "master's tools".[90]

Although Vázquez and Icaza have yet to provide an update on how successful their work was at the University of Amsterdam, it seems to me that their Black Feminist decolonial framework would be effective in incorporating Black British Feminist epistemology within the UK context.

---

[78]ibid 115.
[79]ibid 119.
[80]ibid.
[81]Rutazibwa (n 74) 168.
[82]Icaza and Vázquez (n 75) 119.
[83]ibid 120.
[84]Combahee River Collective (n 4).
[85]ibid; Decolonising SOAS (n 19) 18–19.
[86]Icaza and Vázquez (n 75) 120–21.
[87]Andrews (n 7) 138.
[88]Icaza and Vázquez (n 75) 120–21.
[89]ibid.
[90]Lorde (n 1).

A strategy for Black Feminist decolonisation of curricula in the UK

In the UK many universities are facing up to their past and present roles in sustaining colonial hierarchies.[91] Some of this is due to continued pressure by decolonial student and staff activists, some of whom have explicitly adopted a Black Feminist praxis.[92] Some completely refute the need for decolonisation in the university, and instead view it as "infantilizin[g]" students.[93] However, a Black British feminist decolonisation of British academia does not purport to tell students what to think but rather aims to open up access to a wider array of materials and ideas.

Starting with positionality, within UK law schools, curricula could be interrogated with the question of where does the reading come from?[94] Who created this knowledge and how and why has it been prioritised above other work?[95] As elaborated previously, Black British Feminism interrogates histories of Empire, interrogates issues of socio-economic class, is inherently transnational in nature and has developed, in part, in solidarity with other marginalised groups. Therefore, positionality from a Black British Feminist perspective could mean interrogating curricula through the lens of the British Empire and considering whether or not the curricula perpetuate a colonial narrative. It could also involve interrogating how histories/laws/literature, etc. are connected not only to the British context but to those abroad and particularly how they affect those outside the Western world. Moreover, in a system of higher education where publications and citations are important in the career progression of an academic, it is imperative that decolonisation of the curricula does not just mean having work from the most privileged of an underrepresented group in conversation with hegemonic work. Positionality in this sense also means working to see if voices from the most marginalised groups can be cited and included in classroom conversations, as groups such as Cite Black Women have continued to advocate.[96] This would facilitate decolonisation not only of curricula but also the university as an institution, preventing the continuation of a regressive environment where there has only been a 1.2% increase in the number of Black women becoming professors between 2014 and 2018.[97]

---

[91]Severin Carrell, "Glasgow University to Pay £20m in Slave Trade Reparations" *The Guardian* (London, 23 August 2019) <www.theguardian.com/uk-news/2019/aug/23/glasgow-university-slave-trade-reparations> accessed 16 September 2019; Sally Weale, "Cambridge University to Study How It Profited from Colonial Slavery" *The Guardian* (London, 30 August 2019) <www.theguardian.com/education/2019/apr/30/cambridge-university-study-how-it-profited-colonial-slavery> accessed 16 September 2019; Kenan Malik, "Are Soas Students Right to 'Decolonize' Their Minds from Western Philosophers?" https://www.theguardian.com/education/2017/feb/19/soas-philosopy-decolonise-our-minds-enlightenment-white-european-kenan-malik 16 September 2019.

[92]Decolonising SOAS (n 19) 4; Keele Decolonising the Curriculum Network, "Keele Manifesto for Decolonising the Curriculum" (*Keele University*) <www.keele.ac.uk/equalitydiversity/equalityawards/raceequalitycharter/keeledecolonisingthecurriculumnetwork/#keele-manifesto-for-decolonising-the-curriculum> accessed 16 September 2019.

[93]Wanjiru Njoya and Doug Stokes, "The Misguided Moral Panic about Racism in British Universities" (*Quillette*, 9 February 2020) <https://quillette.com/2020/02/09/the-moral-panic-about-racism-in-british-universities/> accessed 9 February 2020.

[94]Icaza and Vasquez (n 75) 119.

[95]ibid.

[96]As has often been the demand of Black British feminists: see Bryan and others (n 53) 149; Cite Black Women, "Cite Black Women: A Critical Praxis" (*Cite Black Women*) <www.citeblackwomencollective.org/our-praxis.html> accessed 16 September 2019.

[97]Comparing figures cited in Heidi Safia Mirza, "Decolonizing Higher Education: Black Feminism and the Intersectionality of Race and Gender" (2014) (Nos 7/8) Journal of Feminist Scholarship 1, 6 and in Richard Adams, "UK Universities Making Slow Progress on Equality, Data Shows" *The Guardian* (London, 7 September 2018) <https://amp.theguardian.com/education/2018/sep/07/uk-university-professors-black-minority-ethnic> accessed 16 September 2019.

With relationality, we need to encourage the recognition of all student backgrounds as valuable in university classrooms in the UK.[98] This is because the Black Asian and Minority Ethnic (BAME) attainment gap is a very real and long-running problem, where BAME candidates at university are far less likely to get a 2.1 or first class degree compared to their white peers, even if they come into university with the same A Level grades.[99] The attainment gap is a broader issue within the UK education system, particularly for black students. Although some students of immediate black West African descent do better than the national average at GCSE, remaining data suggests that by the time all black children get to age 17/18, regardless of their heritage, they are the group most likely to get a wrong prediction for their A Level grades, affecting the quality of university that they can attend.[100] At university black students are the group least likely to get a 2.1 or a first, with some institutions finding that this is the case even when controlling for socio-economic class.[101] Black students are also more likely to drop out of university than their peers.[102] Therefore, although racial attainment gaps are not just an issue for the university, this is something that the university should do its part to address. This is because universities, and particularly law schools which tend to attract a large number of students, are admitting students who are likely to have been failed in many ways by the education system up until they enrol, as the above data suggests.[103] The university must not be complicit in this by continuing to fail students throughout their studies, and although many university management objectives seem to prioritise construction of infrastructure and economic output, the attainment gap must not be forgotten.

Some academics have tried to dismiss concern over the attainment gap, suggesting that campaigners who want to resolve this issue want a "simple solution" and have erroneously just blamed it on "racism".[104] However, in reality, many, including Universities UK and the National Union of Students, have suggested multiple ways to provide structural change within UK academia, one of which is curriculum reform.[105] Indeed, in their extensive research paper it was detailed that in 2011 42% of BAME students did not "feel that [their] curriculum reflects issues of diversity equality and discrimination. They reported a lack of BAME-specific content and a 'mainstream' way of thinking".[106]

Transforming the curriculum with a Black British Feminist decolonial praxis could potentially help in lessening the attainment gap, particularly if one drew upon the

---

98 Icaza and Vasquez (n 75) 120.

99 Advance HE, "Equality + Higher Education: Students Statistical Report 2018" (*Advance HE*, 6 September 2018) 138 <www.advance-he.ac.uk/sites/default/files/2019-05/2018-06-ECU_HE-stats-report_students_v5-compressed.pdf> accessed 16 September 2019; Richard Adams, "White Students Get Better Degrees than Minority Peers with Same Entry Grades" *The Guardian* <www.theguardian.com/education/2014/mar/28/white-students-better-degrees-minorities-same-grades-universities> accessed 4 May 2020.

100 Jill Rutter, "Back to Basics: Towards a Successful and Cost-Effective Integration Policy" (Institute for Public Policy Research, March 2013) 43; Nick Everett and Joanna Papageorgiou, "Investigating the Accuracy of Predicted A Level Grades as Part of the UCAS Admissions Process" (Department for Business, Innovation and Skills, June 2011).

101 "Black Attainment Gap" (*National Union of Students*) <www.nus.org.uk/en/take-action/education/black-attainment-gap/> accessed 1 May 2020; "The Attainment Gap at LSE" (LSE Students' Union, March 2018) 14–15.

102 Universities UK and the National Union of Students, "Black, Asian and Minority Ethnic Student Attainment at UK Universities: #ClosingtheGap" (May 2019) 7.

103 James Ball, "The Oxford Race Gap: Exploring the Data" *The Guardian* <www.theguardian.com/news/datablog/2013/feb/26/oxford-race-gap-exploring-data> accessed 12 June 2020.

104 Njoya and Stokes (n 93).

105 Universities UK and the National Union of Students (n 102) 17–20.

106 ibid.

importance of solidarity within Black British feminism – facilitating a classroom space in which students do not feel that they are competing with one another, but rather consider they are peers connected through their university experience who each have something useful to contribute. It is important that students feel able to relate subject-matter to their identities and critique it based on their heritage and lived experiences. This is not based on the racist assumption that racialised students cannot relate to white Western icons, as some critics suggest, but rather argues that their attempts to engage with the curricula by relating subject-matter to their heritage, which many racialised students are doing already, should not be demeaned and downgraded.[107] For instance, a black student at Oxford University recently reported being dismissed and disregarded when trying to put scholarship from the Global North in conversation with scholarship from the Global South in his PPE degree.[108] We should ensure that racialised students are not continuing to be treated as "problem people", whose concerns and ideas are extraneous to curricula.[109]

Finally, with regard to transitionality, UK universities should and can critique the knowledge practices of the university and its linkage to harmful socio-political realities.[110] Some universities have already started doing this, but it is important that this takes place inside the classroom as well.[111] While it is true that a university degree is often just a steppingstone to entering a job market where wealth accumulation is the goal, the university is also a transformational space, a space where ideas about reality are produced and reproduced. If we want to transform society, we need to pursue what Black Feminist, bell hooks, calls "education as the practice of freedom", acting and reflecting on the world and what we bring to the world, to challenge and change it for the better.[112] With regard to Black British Feminism, questions like these could be asked: Who does this knowledge embolden and who does it downgrade? How does what we are doing enhance/downgrade a global politic of solidarity? Does this work perpetuate debunked colonial or classist narratives about certain groups? Does it have to? And, how can we rectify this? For example, in intellectual property law, teaching could question why Western conceptualisations of intellectual property mean that indigenous groups cannot copyright their knowledge, thus their knowledge is often co-opted and used for Western profit.[113] Or, in employment law, teaching could ask why at present, our "equality" legislation does not recognise intersectional discrimination, and has a very restrictive list of protected characteristics that has the potential to erase the inequality that some of the most marginalised in our communities face in the workplace.[114]

Legal teaching should not just be about teaching and spoon-feeding pre-proscribed critiques of certain ratios but should itself be introspective, looking at knowledge production in the classroom and asking why certain legal doctrines cause the harm that they do and whether this is reflective of our wider society. By connecting what we

---

[107] Bryan and others (n 53) 170; Icaza and Vázquez (n 75) 120.

[108] Femi Nylander, "SOAS, Philosophy and Oxford Finals" (*feminylander.com*, 11 January 2017) https://www.feminylander.co.uk/single-post/2017/02/06/soas-philosophy-and-oxford-finals accessed 16 September 2019.

[109] Gordon (n 24) 84.

[110] Icaza and Vázquez (n 75) 120.

[111] See references cited in n 91; Icaza and Vázquez (n 75) 120.

[112] bell hooks, *Teaching to Transgress: Education as the Practice of Freedom* (Routledge 1994) 1–14.

[113] Sharmishta Barwa and Shirin M Rai, "Knowledge and/as Power: A Feminist Critique of Trade Related Intellectual Property Rights" (2003) 7 Gender, Technology and Development 91, 104.

[114] Iyiola Solanke, "Infusing the Silos in the Equality Act 2010 with Synergy" (2011) 40 Industrial Law Journal 336.

learn in the classroom to tangible social realities of various groups, and encouraging debate and discourse on them, we will likely no longer have the situation where large numbers of racialised students "don't feel like they belong in academia".[115]

A Black British Feminist dismantling of the master's house is possible and may be a future that we will all bear witness to.

Acknowledgments

Thanks to Dr Foluke Adebisi for always supporting my academic endeavours.

Disclosure statement

No potential conflict of interest was reported by the author.

[115]Anna Fazackerley, "'Look at How White the Academy Is': Why BAME Students Aren't Doing PhDs" <www.theguardian.com/education/2019/sep/12/look-at-how-white-the-academy-is-why-bame-students-arent-doing-phds> accessed 17 September 2019.

The ignored heritage of Western law: the historical and contemporary role of Islamic law in shaping law schools

Imranali Panjwani

ABSTRACT
Whilst Islam's role in shaping science as a whole has been well documented and reasonably recognised, its role in shaping Western law has been almost ignored. Arguably the most famous works on Islam's contribution to Western humanities and law are by George Makdisi but his works are not used as core textbooks in law schools to understand how legal principles and institutions formed within the West. What is worse is that Islamic law is considered as a fringe subject within universities, only relevant to Muslims or specific growth areas such as Islamic finance. Islamic law is not studied for its general jurisprudential value and methods of reasoning despite its ability to be compared to Western jurisprudence. The root of this ignorance by law departments lies in the perception of Islamic law as archaic, incapable of reform and only relevant to minority communities. Nothing could be further from the truth as within the Islamic tradition, much contemporary reform is taking place with a view to reform methods of and interpretations arising from Islamic jurisprudence. My article will examine attitudes towards Islam of Western scholars operating within the field of humanities and law; secondly, to explore the critical historical connections between Islamic law and Western law that have shaped modern legal concepts; and finally, I will share a case study of teaching European Law to demonstrate the damaging effects of a Eurocentric and colonial approach on legal knowledge and the students that learn it. It is hoped that Islamic law is seen not as a relic of the past but as an entity worthy of study and incorporation in our modes of legal reasoning. For this to occur, serious thought needs to be given to decolonising law schools to appreciate the heritage of Islamic law.

Whilst Islam's role in shaping science is well documented and reasonably recognised, its role in shaping Western law has been almost ignored. Arguably the most notable works on Islam's contribution to Western humanities and law are by George Makdisi but his works are not used as core textbooks in law schools to understand how legal principles and institutions formed within the West.[1] What is worse is that Islamic law is considered as a fringe subject within universities, only relevant to Muslims or specific growth areas such as Islamic finance. Islamic law should be studied for its general jurisprudential

[1] George Makdisi, *The Rise of Humanism in Classical Islam and the Christian West: With Special Reference to Scholasticism* (Edinburgh University Press 1990) and *The Rise of Colleges* (Create Space Independent Publishing Platform 2013).

value and methods of reasoning as it is comparable to Western jurisprudence. The root of this ignorance by law departments lies in the perception of Islamic law as archaic, incapable of reform and only relevant to minority communities. However, within the Islamic tradition, much contemporary reform is taking place with a view to reform methods of and interpretations arising from Islamic jurisprudence.

The first part of my article will examine the attitudes towards Islam of Western scholars operating within the field of humanities and law; secondly, I will explore the critical historical connections between Islamic law and Western law that have shaped modern legal concepts; and finally, I will share a case study of teaching European law to demonstrate the damaging effects of a Eurocentric and colonial approach on legal knowledge and the students that learn it. My scholastic approach is directed towards legal scholars, practitioners and students who are unfamiliar with Islamic law. It is therefore hoped that Islamic law is seen not as a relic of the past but as an entity worthy of study and incorporation in our modes of legal reasoning. For this to occur, serious thought needs to be given to decolonising law schools to appreciate the heritage of Islamic law.

What is Islamic law?

Islamic law is a Western term that attempts to describe the various layers of jurisprudence and law in Islam. Muslims themselves, however, state that their "law" comprises six areas:

- Principles of jurisprudence (*usul al-fiqh*), i.e. legal theory
- Jurisprudence (*fiqh*), i.e. applied legal theory
- Jurisprudential maxims (*al-qawaid al-fiqhiyya*), i.e. similar to core legal maxims that guide the application of law
- Rulings (*ahkam*), i.e. similar to primary and secondary legislation and guidelines
- Judgment (*qada*), i.e. a judge's binding judgment in a particular case
- Edicts (*fatawa*): these are issued by jurists and are similar to judges' opinions but do not necessarily carry any enforceability which lies with the individual following them

All of these layers attempt to discover what *shari'ah* is – shari'ah meaning: the way to God or God's ideal regulations that Muslims constantly try to comprehend. Therefore, shari'ah does not mean Islamic law since it comprises rulings that are obligatory (*wajib*) and prohibited (*haram*) and those that are recommended (*mustahab*) and reprehensible (*makruh*). The term "law" means a command that is enforceable in political apparatus,[2] but a ruling of shari'ah may or may not be enforceable and be purely ethical as well. For example, it is obligatory to pray five times a day to God, but a state cannot enforce this against an individual. At the same time, it is obligatory to pay poor-rate tax (*zakat*) which can be enforceable in a Muslim state though unenforceable in a non-Muslim state. It is also recommended for Muslims to greet one another with *salam* (peace) but this is purely ethical in nature. The concept of shari'ah is also all-

[2]"The regime that orders human activities and relations through systematic application of the force of politically organised society, or through social pressure, backed by force, in such a society; the legal system <respect and obey the law> . . . ": Bryan A Garner (ed), *Black's Law Dictionary* (9th edn, West – Thomson Reuters 2009) 962.

encompassing and includes rulings on personal habits, hygiene, dress, and gender interactions as well as performance of rituals, financial transactions, medical procedures, criminal behaviour and war. Therefore, Islamic law is a misleading and restrictive term that does not fully capture the scope and breadth of shari'ah.[3]

Any ruling of Islam is derived in accordance with the procedure of *ijtihad* (the employment of effort to derive a law from its sources: legal reasoning) which is a fallible process of human reasoning to extract law from textual and non-textual sources. Islamic rulings, therefore, are not static but always subject to better reasoning that helps us understand the spirit of the Qur'an and narrations of Prophet Muhammad, his family, and companions. The sources of Islamic rulings are:

- The Qur'an – similar to a constitution that contains the core and overarching principles for human order.
- Narrations (*hadith*) from Prophet Muhammad, his family and companions – similar to historical custom which covers numerous layers from law and morality to ethics and social habits.
- Consensus (*ijma'*) – similar to judges' consensus or accepted precedent that is able to be challenged if valid evidence is found to suggest a different textual interpretation.
- Human intellect (*'aql*)/Analogical reasoning (*qiyas*), i.e. tools of human reasoning that aid our understanding of scripture. This involves the use of human custom (*'urf*) in deriving rational tools as well as norms to interpret scripture, provided they do not contradict it.[4]

The above sources are subject to long-standing jurisprudential disciplines, sophisticated hermeneutical frameworks and the plethora of opinions of jurists. It is not that the sources are examined in a simplistic and non-critical manner; rather, ijtihad is a dynamic process of interpreting textual sources using both linguistic and rational argumentation. These modes of reasoning are comparable to the conceptual categories of law, the approaches to interpreting statute, use of historical and present-day custom and precedent and obiter dicta of judges in English law. Whilst the focus of this article is more historical, a few examples suffice here to demonstrate this dynamism.

Usul al-fiqh or legal theory is defined by the well-known Shi'i jurist, whose works continue to be studied today, Mohammed Baqir al-Sadr (d. 1980), as:

> Indeed the subject-matter of the science of the principles [of jurisprudence] is everything that is anticipated to be an evidence and common element in the procedure of derivation of the religious law and the argumentation for it.[5]

[3]See the analysis by Fatemi, "by labelling fiqhi norms as 'law', however, he contributes to the confusion about the nature of fiqh, a confusion created by previous scholars such as Schacht in their introductions to the discipline (Schacht, 1964). As I have concluded elsewhere, fiqh should not be confused either with 'law' in the modern sense or with a 'moral system' in modern philosophical terms (Fatemi, 2005a, p. 298). Fiqhi norms are a set of religious ethical commands and precepts with rare legal sanctions that are a product of jurists' argumentation from primary sources of Shari'ah (Fatemi, 2005b, p. 194.)": S Mohammad Ghari Fatemi, "Autonomy and Equal Right to Divorce with Specific Reference to Shi'i Fiqh and the Iranian Legal System" (2006) 17 Islam and Christian-Muslim Relations 281, 282–83.

[4]For a more detailed analysis of the nature of Islamic law, see Muhammad Baqir al-Sadr. *Principles of Islamic Jurisprudence: According to Shi'i Law* (Arif Abdulhussein tr, ICAS Press 2003) and Wael B Hallaq, *The Origins and Evolution of Islamic Law* (Cambridge University Press 2005).

[5]Muḥammad Baqir al-Sadr, *Durus fi 'ilm al-usul – al-Halaqat al-thaniya* (Majma' al-fikr al-islami 1992) 20.

This contemporary definition of legal theory, which contrasts with the earlier definitions of the discipline in which some Muslim scholars stated that the subject-matter should be only the four sources of the Qur'an, narrations, consensus and intellect, shows a distinct broadening in the usage of evidence to derive laws of shari'ah. A common element is the "commonness of the usefulness of a component in entering the derivation of a ruling in any instance amongst the instances which the jurist encounters . . . like the imperative verbal form being apparent in obligation".[6] This means that a common element cannot be a specific component that has a self-contained subject-matter. Rather it is a general principle such as the authority of the apparent meaning (*hujjiyat al-dhawahir*) that can be applied to specific issues. The example he gives is the apparentness of the imperative verbal form from which the meaning of obligation can be deduced, and so several obligations can be derived from the imperative verbal form such as the obligation of prayer and fasting. This also allows procedural principles (*al-usul al-amaliyya*) to be introduced; a procedural principle outlines the practical standpoint in performing a duty in the absence of scriptural evidence.[7]

Sadr's and other Muslim jurists' approach to legal theory shows an expansion of the linguistic and rational sources that can be used to derive a ruling of shari'ah which are not exclusively based on scripture.[8] This hermeneutical approach has similarities to the literal, golden, mischief and purposive rule in English law in trying to find the intent of the legislator and what to do in cases where there is a gap or mischief in the legislation or a particular mode of interpretation leads to absurdity and conflict in the nature of law and its application.[9]

In addition to the above, jurisprudential maxims (*al-qawaid al-fiqhiyyah*) aid the jurist in deriving jurisprudential rules. "A jurisprudential maxim contains a general religious ruling that from its application can be used to obtain a specific religious ruling in a particular case",[10] whereas usul al-fiqh or legal theory constitutes the theoretical source or common elements from which jurisprudential maxims can be derived. For example, the maxim of purity (*qa'idat al-taharah*) states "if a person doubts the purity or impurity of a thing then it is deemed to be pure".[11] Or the maxim of averting hardship (*qa'idat nafy al-haraj*) which is "the negation of every ruling, that if it were to be established, would necessitate hardship on the worshippers".[12] This means rules of shari'ah that lead to hardship are set aside in cases of extreme difficulty. The content and operation of Islamic jurisprudential maxims are very similar to English legal maxims that judges use to aid their application of legislation in case law.[13]

---

[6]ibid 18.

[7]ibid.

[8]See also Muḥammad Rida al-Muzaffar, *Usul al-fiqh* (Isma liyyan 2010) 1:10–11. The maqasid discourse is also important to understanding how Sunni jurisprudence provides answers to contemporary issues. See Imranali Panjwani, "Book Review: Shari'a in the Modern Era: Muslim Minorities Jurisprudence by Iyad Zahalka" (2017) 34 American Journal of Islamic Social Sciences 114.

[9]Glanville Williams, *Learning the Law* (15th edn, Sweet & Maxwell 2013) 124–46.

[10]Baqir al-Irwani, *Durus Tamhidiyya fi al-Qawaid al-Fiqhiyya* (2 vols) (Majma' al-Nashirin 2014) vol 1, 16. Irwani's book has been translated into English by Zaid Alsalami as: *Introduction to Jurisprudential Maxims* (ICAS Press 2017).

[11]ibid 33.

[12]ibid 137.

[13]George Frederick Wharton, *Legal Maxims with Observations and Cases* (1878) <http://rodscontracts.com/docs/legal/LegalMaximsWithCaseCites.pdf> accessed 12 July 2020.

The definitions of legal theory and jurisprudential maxims show critical debate taking place within Muslim scholarship as to the purpose and scope of Islamic law, particularly for contemporary situations which have not been explicitly legislated by the Qur'an or narrations. It is also common to find edicts on bioethics, end-of-life issues, plastic surgery as well as more mundane affairs that have been affected by science such as sighting of the moon which can be done using an optical aid or astronomical calculations.[14] The issues of human dignity, slavery, interfaith marriage, the role of a woman in modern society, the permissibility of financial transactions within a society that operates on *riba* (interest) and more continue to be debated in Muslim seminaries, particularly in more reformist quarters.[15]

Ultimately, Islamic rulings regulate all aspects of Muslims' personal and public lives and are arguably the most important area in their lives as Muslims always want to know whether their actions are valid in the eyes of God. For the purposes of making this article accessible to a wider base of academics and scholars only, I will use the term "Islamic law" but with the intricacies I have outlined above.

The last century: a summary of the attitudes towards Islam and Islamic law

Whilst there are certainly more voices than before speaking for the contribution of Islam as a religion and its sciences to human civilisation, there is still a perception that these sciences do not have an enduring place within Western humanities departments; rather they should be confined to either Muslim seminaries or Islamic Studies departments within Western universities.[16] What has caused this separation between "Islam and the West" from the perspective of intellectual history?[17] An appropriate starting point is perhaps Sir Hamilton Gibb's (1895–1971) lecture in 1955 about the influence of Islamic culture on medieval Europe. Gibb was then Professor of Arabic at the University of Oxford. He stated:

> On the whole, therefore, the contributions to the west from Arabic sources, although at first some of them seemed to be alien and dangerous, tended ultimately to reinforce the medieval Catholic culture rather than to disturb it. I see no argument for the assumption, still fairly often made, that these importations in themselves struck at the roots of medieval thought and prepared the way for its overthrow, with the one possible exception of Averrorism – but this itself had become stagnant and inert by the end of the fourteenth century.[18]

His statement is telling, if not fundamentally ignorant about the nature and transmission of Islam in Western Europe. The idea that Arabic sources are "alien and dangerous" stems from the perception that Islam is monolithic, inflexible, barbaric, aggressive, intolerant and incapable of interacting with other civilisations. This has its roots in the

[14]In terms of Sunni scholarship, see the opinions of the European Council for Fatwa and Research presided over by Yusuf al-Qaradawi <www.sistani.org/arabic/book/17/956/> accessed 23 June 2020 and its English translation: *A Code of Practice for Muslims in the West* <www.sistani.org/english/book/46/> accessed 23 June 2020.

[15]See the innovative fiqh workshops and publications of the Al-Mahdi Institute in Birmingham, UK founded by Shaykh Arif Abdulhussain <www.usuli.org/> accessed 12 July 2020.

[16]See Ataullah Siddiqui, "Islam at Universities in England" (The Siddiqui Report, 2007) <www.mihe.org.uk/the-siddiqui-report> accessed 15 October 2019.

[17]For an analysis of these attitudes, see Humberto Garcia, *Islam and the English Enlightenment 1670–1840* (The Johns Hopkins University Press 2011).

[18]Hamilton Gibb, "The Influence of Islamic Culture on Medieval Europe" (1955) 38 Bulletin of the John Rylands Library 82, 98.

seventh century when many Christians feared that Islam would rival the status of Christianity as a dominant world religion. St John Damascene, the seventh-century monk and priest who was "the real founder of the Christian tradition [against Islam]",[19] claimed that the Qur'an imitated the Old and the New Testaments incompletely and that this was to "become a pillar of Christian accusations against Islam as a false religion in the centuries to come".[20] This mistrust was heightened in al-Andalus; while some form of *convivencia* was enjoyed there, it also had its fair share of tensions. There, some of the Christian clergy attacked the "Muslim Prophet as a licentious Arab who promoted lust in the form of polygamous commandment".[21] The Crusades accelerated the derogatory image of Islam: "the image of a savage, dark-skinned Saracen, the pagan enemy of Jesus Christ, did not appear merely as papal propagation to keep the flames of war high; nor was it meant to address the crusaders only; soon after the First Crusades, it entered Christian art and literature, a space in its imagination."[22]

Gibb also plays down the importance of Averrorism, i.e. the work of the famed Muslim jurist and philosopher, Ibn Rushd (1126–1198). Rather as Runciman argues, Roger Bacon of Oxford stated that philosophy must be learnt from the Arabic writers and that no one should study the subject without taking the trouble to learn Oriental languages. And John of Salisbury reminds his readers of the debt owed to Muslim philosophers. Indeed, a few of Aristotle's works and almost all of Plato's came to the West directly from the Greeks of Byzantium but the philosophical works that affected Western thought most deeply came in translations from the Arabic, enriched by the comments made by Muslim philosophers – specifically Ibn Sina (980–1037) known as Avicenna in the West and Ibn Rushd.[23]

Later, Western philosophers when they could read Greek realised just how much their interpretation of Aristotle and Plato had been influenced by Muslims. Indeed, Thomas Aquinas whose work still forms the basis of the philosophical doctrine of the Catholic Church tried to disentangle Aristotelian philosophy from Muslim philosophy and attempted to add in his system elements direct from Plato. However, his methods show distinct Muslim influences. For example, his interplay between faith and reason appears to have been copied from Ibn Rushd and his attitude to the Bible is that of Ibn Rushd's attitude to the Qur'an. Both believe God's word was supreme authority but could be explained in Aristotelian philosophical terms. Ultimately, Aquinas concluded that science was not incompatible with religion – the same conclusion reached by Ibn Rushd.[24]

Despite Runciman's and others' appreciation of Ibn Sina's and Ibn Rushd's contribution to philosophy and theology, Gibb admits not having read Aquinas' *Summa Theologica*. He then casually concludes that it is a "masterpiece" whereas the works of al-Farabi, Avicenna and Averroes are masterpieces but in "different degrees":

[19]Saied Reza Ameli, *Bibliographical Discourse Analysis: The Western Academic Perspective on Islam, Muslims and Islamic Countries (1949–2009) Volumes 1–4* (Islamic Human Rights Commission 2012) vol 1, 20–21.

[20]ibid.

[21]ibid 23.

[22]ibid 28.

[23]See Steven Runciman, "Muslim Influences on the Development of European Civilization" (1959) 3 Sarkiyat Mecmuasi 13 <https://dergipark.org.tr/en/download/article-file/10445> accessed 7 October 2019.

[24]ibid and see Averroes, *Decisive Treatise and Epistle Dedicatory* (Charles E Butterworth tr and ed with Introduction and Notes, Brigham Young University Press 2001) 1–8.

> The *Summa* (which I have not read, and do not expect ever to read) is, no doubt, a masterpiece of creative synthesis; but so, in different degrees, are the writings of al-Farabi, Avicenna and Averroes.[25]

It is precisely this presumptuous attitude towards Islamic sciences that has resulted in its contribution being downplayed within Western humanities. A shift, however, did occur in the 1970s with the realisation that non-Western civilisations had much more to offer than what the Western world was claiming. This was concomitant with the rise of intellectually rigorous voices such as those of George Makdisi and Edward Said who started to thoroughly investigate the origins of Western universities, their teaching methods and conception of humanities from their historical and geographical links with Muslim lands as well as their perception of the Orient.

Consider the following statement by Berman which correctly questions the validity of Western laws for non-Western cultures and attempts to view the Western legal tradition in a "large historical perspective":[26]

> In the past, Western man has confidently carried his law with him throughout the world. The world today, however, is more suspicious than ever before of Western "legalism." Eastern man and Southern man offer other alternatives. The West itself has come to doubt the universal validity of its vision of law – its validity for non-Western cultures.[27]

However, he fails to articulate what this perspective should be. He only briefly mentions Buddhist, Chinese and Confucian thought and completely omits any mention of Islam or its legal tradition.[28] Whilst claiming to examine the "religious foundations" of the Western legal tradition, his major focus is on Christianity and its worldview.

He further argues that approximately in the year 1100, the first modern law school was founded in the town of Bologna in Northern Italy. Students came from all over Europe to study law as a distinct and coherent body of knowledge, a science separate from politics and separate from religion. The law that was studied here was from an ancient manuscript from the enormous collection of legal materials which had been compiled under the Roman Emperor Justinian in Constantinople in about AD 534, almost six centuries earlier. It was this body of law that formed the object of Europe's first systematic legal studies.[29]

However, his aforementioned analysis contradicts his earlier point that between the sixth and tenth centuries, Roman law barely survived in the West, although it continued to flourish in the Eastern Empire.[30] How did "scholasticism", i.e. a professional class of scholars engaging in formal teaching, research and critique come about when Roman law barely survived in Europe? It appears unlikely that almost out of nothing the Western legal tradition developed into the system that it is today. This is precisely the point which Boisard makes, that academic treaties of law were translated in Italy from Arab texts and circulated in Europe which influenced the teaching and making of law.[31]

The paradigm of Western scholars has been to view Islam through a Judeo-Christian and Greco-Roman lens rather than using Islam's own sources to understand its development. As proof, Ameli's research strikes at the heart of how the West has viewed Islam since the

[25] Gibb (n 18) 93.
[26] Harold J Berman, "The Religious Foundations of Western Law" (1975) 24 Cath U L Rev 490, 490 <http://scholarship.law.edu/lawreview/vol24/iss3/4> accessed 7 October 2019.
[27] ibid.
[28] ibid 503–04.
[29] ibid 491–92.
[30] ibid.
[31] Marcel A Boisard, "On the Probable Influence of Islam on Western Public and International Law" (1980) 11 Int J Middle East Stud 429, 440.

seventh century. He samples 23,872 items of books and articles that cover the period from 1949 to 2009 discussing how Western scholars have feared, ignored, or downplayed the role of Islam in the development of Western civilisation. It is here that the most interesting discourse is analysed, "Islamoromia". Works in this category contextualise Islam in the bosom of the Roman tradition embodying the West in general and compare Islam with and in a Western mindset pronouncing their favour for Western values as superior to Islamic ones.[32]

Works in this section not only represent the highest percentage of all the discourses (11,563 items constituting 48.4% of the total) but show that Islam and its sciences are seen as inferior to Western sciences. They are not analysed for their own merit and what they have contributed and can contribute to civilisation today; rather they are always seen through the prism of a "superior" Western scholastic tradition. Islam is, as Nasr argues, a "religion seen in constant conflict and war"[33] and "only the most external aspects of the religion came to be taught"[34] in academic institutions.

We can reasonably conclude that Western scholars over the course of last century have not been kind to the contribution of Muslim jurists and philosophers to their own history. Certainly, there have been exceptions to this norm and some of the contemporary writings that are emerging demonstrate a realisation of the closer links between Islamic and Western history. The fact remains, however, that Islamic law has unfortunately been regarded as having its own historical timeline that is disconnected from Western legal development.

The influence of Islamic legal scholasticism on Western law schools

According to Makdisi, two movements dominate the intellectual history of Islam – humanism and scholasticism, and both are tied to the Qur'an.[35] The rise of these two movements gradually influenced Europe or what he terms the "Christian West", which covers the period from the seventh to the fourteenth centuries.[36]

Within Islamic legal scholarship, Makdisi is clearly recognised as a rigorous and towering scholar who made a unique contribution in tracing the roots of Western humanities, law and educational institutions to Islamic sciences, Muslim lands and the methods and institutions that developed there.[37] However, Makdisi's scholarship has only been recognised by scholars within the field of Islamic law and Islamic studies. The journals in which his work has been critically reviewed such as *Islamic Law and Society*, *Journal of Islamic Studies* and *Journal of the Royal Asiatic Society* are prestigious, but his work has not been taken seriously or influenced mainstream Western legal journals, scholars, law departments, law curricula and legal institutions.[38]

---

[32]Ameli, *Bibliographical Discourse Analysis* (n 19) 49.

[33]Mumtaz Ahmed, Zahid Bukhar and Sulayman Nyang (eds), *Observing the Observer: The State of Islamic Studies in American Universities* (International Institute of Islamic Thought 2012) 15.

[34]ibid.

[35]Makdisi, *The Rise of Humanism in Classical Islam* (n 1) xix.

[36]ibid xx.

[37]Jonathan P Berkey, "Reviewed Work: Makdisi, George. Religion, Law and Learning in Classical Islam. Collected Studies Series CS 347. London: Variorum" (1997) 4 Islamic Law and Society 242, 242–43 <www.jstor.org/stable/pdf/3399496.pdf?refreqid=excelsior%3A1583f5aa8b61dc53737306fe4fb6a1b1> accessed 26 June 2020.

[38]See for example Gary Slapper and David Kelly, *The English Legal System: 2014-2015* (Routledge 2014) and *English Law* (Routledge 2009) by the same authors; Williams, *Learning the Law* (n 9) and James Penner and Emmanuel Melissaris, *McCoubrey & White's Textbook on Jurisprudence* (Oxford University Press 2012) amongst many others. To its credit, *McCoubrey & White's Textbook on Jurisprudence* mentions the nature of Islamic law on pages 21–22, but this lacks sufficient detail and is disconnected from the other jurisprudential theories in the book as if Islamic jurisprudence is a separate and distinct entity in itself.

There is now at least some recognition within pockets of Western academia that there is an urgent need to take Muslim scholarship more seriously for the relationship is "far more complex than at first appears"[39] and "if some important European legal institutions that emerged in the early Middle Ages have at least some Islamic origins, this area of transmission and reception has potentially important implications for understanding the emergence of the modern state and governance in Europe".[40]

It is known that Islamic influence on the Christian Latin West existed in fields such as philosophy and medicine because of the translation of books in those sciences from Arabic to Latin as well as adoption of Arabic terms. However, it is generally not known that the books in the field of humanistic studies such as law have also been translated from Arabic to Latin and other European languages and that terms of humanism in the West are terms of classical Arabic humanism.

For example, the closeness of the term "guild" denoting a kind of fraternity which would form the basis of the legal schools and inns in Europe is striking. The Arabic terms of *hirfa, ta'ifa, tariqa, sinf* would later be replicated in the West through the terms of confraternity, brotherhood, craft, *metier*, corporation, *hanse, jurande*, guild (gild). No one denies that guilds existed in Islam at the end of the Middle Ages, but did they exist prior to this period, specifically in the ninth to eleventh centuries? Makdisi answers in the affirmative. During the ninth century, juridical *madhabs* (schools) began to exist; in the tenth century, mosques-colleges began to exist and then by the eleventh century, Muslim jurists and legal schools reached the height of their development with a clear-cut structure. Examples of the early juridical madhabs were those of the Iraqis, Madanis, Basrawis and Kufians. These became legal schools after their founders which have survived today – Shafi'i (after Muhammad ibn Idris al-Shafiʿi, 767–820), Hanbali (after Ahmed ibn Hanbal, 780–855), Hanafi (after Abu Hanifa, 699–767), Maliki (after Malik ibn Anas, 711–795) and Ja'fari (after Ja'far al-Sadiq, 702–765).[41]

The crystallisation of the Islamic legal schools led to the creation of formal designations capable of expressing juridical authority and studying Islamic jurisprudence. For example, the *mutafaqqih* in Islam arguably gave rise to the notion of *escolatre* in France and scholar in England. In Islam, *sahib* was used denoting *bachelier* in France and fellow in England. Finally, the term *mufti/mudarris* may have given rise to the term *magister/maire* in France and *magister*/master in England. There are two arguments to support the notion that Islamic legal scholasticism provides the structure upon which the latter legal schools in the West were built.[42]

First, the institution of the *waqf* (charitable endowment) in Islam appears to have provided the foundation for the English charitable trust which led to the formation of universities and legal schools. Indeed, as Gaudiosi argues,

---

[39]Lisa Watanabe, "The Possible Contribution of Islamic Legal Institutions to the Emergence of a Rule of Law and the Modern State in Europe" in Nayef RF Al-Rodhan (ed), *The Role of the Arab-Islamic World in the Rise of the West* (Palgrave Macmillan 2012) 61 <https://doi.org/10.1057/9780230393219_4> accessed 26 June 2020.

[40]ibid.

[41]Makdisi, *The Rise of Humanism in Classical Islam* (n 1) 15–21.

[42]ibid 15. There are also many examples of Latin maxims about law that appear to have originated from the Qur'an and Prophetic narrations. For example, the axiom *pacta sunt servanda* (agreements must be kept) resembles the first verse of Surat al-Ma'idah, "ufu bi al-'uqud" (keep your agreements). See also Boisard (n 31).

> Oxford University would seem to represent the quintessential English academic institution. Yet, in its early phases of development, Oxford may have owed much to the Islamic legal institution of *waqf* (pl. *awqaf*), charitable trust.[43]

Waqf is the detention of the corpus from the ownership of any person and the gift of its income or usufruct either at present or in the future, to some charitable purpose. The basic principles of a waqf are that it is: irrevocable, perpetual and inalienable – meaning it cannot be sold or made the subject of a mortgage, gift, inheritance or any kind of disposition. Additionally, a waqf could not violate Islamic law – for example, the construction of a church or synagogue or propagating any activities against the core tenets of Islam. A waqf would be composed of the *waqif* (owner of the trust) and *mutawalli* (trustee). And a *qadi* (judge) would oversee its jurisdiction and ensure that beneficiaries are enjoying the rights granted to them under it.

The concept of the waqf led to the creation of the "masjid-college", i.e. a mosque that offers lessons and courses to students intending to learn Islamic law and Islamic sciences in general. Apart from religious worship, mosques were a foundational place for learning and educational activity to the extent that today, in Egypt, Iraq, Iran and other places in the Middle East, a central mosque is adjacent to a madrasah or *hawza* (seminary) or its courtyard is used for teaching and discussion circles. Today, Lincoln's Inn, Inner Temple, Middle Temple and Gray's Inn all follow the above format – the existence of a chapel, classrooms, library and the notion that perpetual legal education would be provided to all those interested and eligible.[44] However, as Gaudiosi argues, the admission that the original waqf and legal school structure within Muslim lands influenced the endowments and legal schools in the West is dismissed and instead, traced to Roman and/or Germanic origins.[45]

Jerusalem was a key point of contact between England and the Islamic world because of the presence of the Orders of the Templars and Hospitallers there. These orders were religious and/or military organisations active during the Crusades. According to Gaudiosi, these religious orders appear to have been quite influential in the development of the Inns of Court in fourteenth-century England.[46]

We can plausibly argue that the travel and contact of Europeans in Muslim lands led to them being influenced by Islamic legal institutions. The crusader states, commerce with Italian cities and perhaps most importantly, the treaties between Muslim rulers and Christian naval powers which developed a kind of Mediterranean naval trade law that was based on pre-Islamic law are all significant points of contact between Europeans and Muslims.[47] It is therefore not surprising that the similarity between the waqf and the English charitable trust is striking: property is reserved, usufruct appropriated for the benefit of specific individuals or general charitable purpose; corpus inalienable; estates for life in favour of successive beneficiaries can be created without regard to the law of

---

[43]Monica M Gaudiosi, "The Influence of the Islamic Law of Waqf on the Development of the Trust in England: The Case of Merton College" (1988) 136 University of Pennsylvania Law Review 1231, 1231.

[44]Cecil Headlam, "The Inns of Court" (Project Gutenberg, 2017): <https://www.gutenberg.org/files/55062/55062-h/55062-h.htm> accessed accessed 4 October 2020.

[45]Gaudiosi, "The Influence of the Islamic Law of Waqf" (n 43) 1240 and see William Holdsworth, *A History of English Law* (3rd edn, Methuen 1945) 410–11.

[46]Gaudiosi, "The Influence of the Islamic Law of Waqf" (n 43) 1245.

[47]See Richard Potz, "Islamic Law and the Transfer of European Law" (2011) European History Online <https://d-nb.info/1036230066/34> accessed 9 October 2019.

inheritance or the rights of heirs and continuity is secured by the successive appointment of trustees.

The second argument is about the teaching, academic freedom and debate that went on inside the waqfs or specifically, Islamic legal schools. Historians of the Latin Christian West have traced the doctorate of the modern university back to the medieval "licence to teach", called in Latin, *licentia docendi*. The issue however is that this was arguably not a product of ancient Greece or ancient Rome as it would have come into conflict with existing teaching authority and the magisterium of the ecclesiastical hierarchy. Muslim lands (for example, Madinah, Makkah, Iraq) in the eighth to ninth centuries, however, had begun to develop the *ijazat al-tadris* (the licence to teach).[48] Before *licentia docendi* appeared in the Christian West, they had developed the magisterium which is the perennial, authentic and infallible teaching office committed to the Apostles by Christ and now possessed and exercised by their legitimate successors, the college of bishops in union with the pope. So now how could a professor of theology obtain a licence to teach and claim independence from the magisterium?

The licence to teach was arguably an intrusive element in Christianity; rather the licence to teach developed from the individualistic learning system of Islamic sciences, not the ecclesiastical hierarchy of Christianity, nor Judaism where the high authority of the Gaon was recognised (major seat of learning of Jewish world in Babylon (Iraq).[49] There are certainly some similarities with Judaism but it did not encourage seeking an opinion from more than one Rabbi. Within Muslim learning, students and laymen were encouraged to seek opinions from various muftis and make their free choice – a hallmark trait that has remained today in the Muslim world. Indeed, Islamic legal schools themselves became authoritative but allowed the emerging jurists to develop ijtihad in their own manner without being answerable to a higher authority. The *mujtahid* (jurist) or mufti could then issue a legal opinion which a layman could choose to follow or not. Moreover, each mujtahid was independent of the others, was not bound to follow anyone else and could dissent against other opinions, even a consensus. The intricate development of legal teaching and authority within the context of independent research and academic freedom not only formed the basis of the classical Islamic legal schools but had a profound effect on the legal schools that emerged in the West in the twelfth to thirteenth centuries after European merchants came into contact with Muslim scholars and their institutions.[50]

Therefore, the nature of waqf in Islam, its usage to create legal schools and the independent way in which law was taught offer a more reliable thesis for the formation of legal schools in the West than the survival of their own remote literature that was hardly followed by their own scholars. It is arguable, as Jokisch comments, that the confrontation with Islamic law not only initiated the Western re-discovery of Roman law in the eleventh century but that in particular the latter's scholasticism through the connection with Aristotelian logic can be traced back to Islamic models. Consequently, nearly every literary genre of mediaeval learned law could already be found in the writings of Islamic jurists.[51]

---

[48]Makdisi, *The Rise of Humanism in Classical Islam* (n 1) 24.
[49]ibid 28.
[50]ibid 24–36 and Boisard (n 31) 439.
[51]Potz (n 47) and see Nayef RF Al-Rodhan, *The Role of the Arab-Islamic World in the Rise of the West: Implications for Contemporary Trans-Cultural Relations* (Palgrave Macmillan 2012).

The effects of Eurocentrism and colonisation on law syllabuses: a case study of European Union law

The damaging effects of teaching law using textbooks and journal articles that are not only Eurocentric but historically inaccurate cannot be ignored. Dismissing the contribution of Islamic legal heritage in the origins and development of Western law leads students to believe that it is only within Western legal and philosophical sources that answers can be found to solve problems in the world. Instead of embracing what non-Western legal sources have to offer, the immediate mentality of students is to relegate these sources to the community, country or religious group that uses them, to be cautious of these sources or to dismiss them altogether. My own teaching experiences not only confirm this but show that Muslims' experience of war, their perceived identity in Europe and their contribution to and interaction with European law has been minimised and neglected.

I teach EU law to second year students and read the introductions to four major EU law textbooks. These were: *European Union Law* by Catherine Barnard and Steve Peers (2017), *European Law* by John Fairhurst (2016), *Complete EU Law* by Berry, Homewood and Bogusz (2019) and *European Union Law* by Horspool, Humphreys and Wells-Greco (2018). All of the introductions had the following reasons in common as to why the European Union formed. First, European countries wanted to reduce the threat of wars and conquests after World War II in order to foster unity amongst them. Secondly, they wanted to control coal and steel so that it would not fall in the hands of a dictator. Thirdly, they wanted to benefit economically from each other by agreeing upon free movement of goods, persons, capital and services. These reasons highlight Europe's common civilisation, moral progress and political and economic integration which stem from their Greek and Roman heritage – a narrative touted by Horspool, Humphreys and Wells-Greco:

> The idea of a "united Europe" has a long history. "Europe" was already conceived of as an entity in Greek and Roman times. Roman citizenship is often taken as the inspiration for the modern idea of European citizenship. It was Cicero, himself a lawyer, who claimed that the proudest boast of an individual in the Roman Empire was *civis Romanus sum*, and the aspiration is that one day the European citizen will regard the accolade of European citizenship with the same respect and pride, as Advocate General Jacobs said in Case C-168/91 *Konstantinidis v Stadt Altensteig* (1993): *civis Europeus sum* [...]. The modern ideal is based on the idea of a common civilisation, common origins, a common spiritual heritage, and common ways of thinking. Philosophies and spiritual ideas always transcended national borders, as do science, culture, painting, music and so on. In Roman times, in the Middle Ages, and subsequently, free movement of persons was something to which at least educated people were accustomed, but others, too, travelled surprisingly widely. Obstacles to such travel, and to the free movement of goods, date from relatively recently. The concept of a unified Europe has been put into practice on several later occasions to a greater or lesser extent, but it has never endured. Before the twentieth century, however, conquest was generally the driving force behind attempts at unification.[52]

This traditional narrative can, however, be critiqued. First, the aforementioned textbooks do not consider the European Union's continuing colonial legacy and specifically,

[52]Margot Horspool, Matthew Humphreys and Michael Wells-Greco, *European Union Law* (10th edn, Oxford University Press 2018) 1–2.

how its ability to economically progress has depended upon its forceful acquisition of other countries' resources, their labour and campaign against resisting groups.[53]

The Algerian War (1954–1962) is a specific example of the then Economic Community's continuing abuse of human rights. The war, which claimed some 1.5 million Algerian lives, saw French forces (approximately 500,000) crack down on independence fighters in the colony ruled by Paris for 130 years.[54] The war was incredibly brutal and demonstrated the French state's systematic utilisation of torture despite the fact that colonial Algeria was officially just as much a part of France as for example, Brittany.[55]

European Union law textbooks do not mention the Algerian War because it conflicts with their narrative of the European Union as a bastion of "peace and progress". Indeed, in their timeline, 1957 was when the Treaty of Rome was signed by Belgium, France, Italy, Luxembourg, the Netherlands and West Germany to create the European Economic Community (EEC). This treaty was the basis of the formation of the European common market and customs union which enabled the free movement of people, goods, capital and services. It is ironic that at the same time that the EEC was formed, France was torturing and killing Algerian people and denying "free movement of people" within its own territory. The same can be said of the United Kingdom's abuse of human rights: Dixon and McCorquodale comment that prior to its incorporation of the European Convention on Human Rights (ECHR), the UK had a "dismal record" of protecting human rights.[56] The fact that a European country signs a treaty or adopts a human rights convention does not wipe away its colonial history nor does it guarantee that its colonial actions would not continue in the future. It is this separatist approach to European history, law and human rights that creates the dichotomised student.[57]

Secondly, the notion of free movement of goods, persons, capital and services that are regulated by commercial treaties resembles more the decrees and laws initiated by Muslim sultans in the thirteenth to fifteenth centuries to regulate foreign trade. For example, the 1489 treaty between the Republic of Florence and Mamluk Sultan Qa'itba appears more as a decree from the Sultan to his administration in Egypt and Syrian Levant rather than as a bilateral reciprocal international instrument binding the two parties. The "treaty" shows customs taxes, admin fees, ways of settling credits and establishment of a consul among merchants. This commercial treaty adheres closely to Islamic law.[58] Another example is the Consulate of the Sea in 1340 where research shows that it was not merely by chance that the Consulate blossomed in a region of the world that was most sensitive to exterior influence and Muslim domination. It would be unfair to ascribe to pure coincidence that such a convention corresponding to "classical" Islamic laws and practices appeared in this region of Europe, one which was the

---

[53] Peo Hansen, "European Integration, European Identity and the Colonial Connection" (2002) 5 European Journal of Social Theory 483, 487.

[54] "France Admits Use of Torture During Algerian War of Independence" (*Al Jazeera*, 13 September 2018) <https://www.aljazeera.com/news/2018/9/13/france-admits-torture-during-algerias-war-of-independence> accessed 12 July 2020.

[55] ibid.

[56] Martin Dixon and Robert McCorquodale, *Cases and Materials on International Law* (Oxford University Press 2003) 122.

[57] For a detailed exposition on how binaries are created in the mind through epistemic genocide, see Ramon Grosfoguel, "The Structure of Knowledge in Westernized Universities: Epistemic Racism/Sexism and the Four Genocides/Epistemicides of the Long 16th Century" (2013) 11(1) Human Architecture: Journal of the Sociology of Self-Knowledge 73.

[58] Boisard (n 31) 433.

most influenced by Muslim culture; moreover, up to the end of the fifteenth century, most of the commercial routes crossed Muslim lands.[59]

What is important to appreciate is how Islamic law may have stimulated conceptions of trade, movement and international relations within Europe. As Boisard argues,

> To try and synthesize the contribution of Islam would be impossible, since it was first of all *the image that humanity provided* that later stimulated the development of international law in the Christian West. It would not be possible, however, to separate this kind of approach from the whole. It suffices to emphasize that Grotius, the founder of "public international law," lived in the seventeenth century, whereas Shaybani, who wrote a treatise at least as complete and systematic, taking into account the generally casuistical presentation of Muslim law, died at the beginning of the ninth![60]

Thirdly, the notion that the European Union is based upon geographical unity and intends for all within this vicinity to prosper economically is false. As proof, there are places in South America and North Africa that form part of the European Union because they were former colonies of France and Spain respectively. These places are of course not in Europe but benefit from rights similar to those of European citizens. For example, the four French Overseas Departments of Réunion, Guyana, Martinique and Guadeloupe and Spanish possessions in North Africa, Melilla and Ceuta, are all as much part of the EU as are metropolitan France and Spain. The inhabitants of these places are in fact citizens of the EU and have voting rights in EU Parliament elections and the right to free movement. One could argue that they are actually more integrated into the EU than perceived European countries such as Sweden, Denmark and Great Britain.[61]

Therefore, there is no geographical unity if places in South America and North Africa form part of the European Union (even if indirectly) whilst Morocco's application in 1987 to the then European Community was rejected on the basis of a lack of geographical closeness. We may then ask, what is "Europe"? If it is not completely based on geographical closeness, then is it based on a common culture? Or is it based upon the acceptance of certain socio-political norms defined by European masters that have dictated the colonisation of others for centuries? A case in point is Turkey. Turkey has been a candidate member since 1987, but it has been criticised by most European states as abusing human rights. In turn, Turkey has criticised European states for their past and present human rights abuses such as the Algerian War, European states supplying weapons to terrorist countries and their continuing support for invasions in the Middle East.[62] The Copenhagen criteria determine whether Turkey or any state can join the EU. Specifically,

> Membership requires that the candidate country has achieved stability of institutions guaranteeing democracy, the rule of law, human rights and respect for and protection of minorities, the existence of a functioning market economy as well as the capacity to cope with competitive pressure and market forces within the Union. Membership presupposes the candidate's ability to take on the obligations of membership including adherence to the aims of political, economic and monetary union.[63]

---

[59]ibid.
[60]ibid 447–48.
[61]Hansen (n 53) 488–89.
[62]Emiliano Alessandri, Ian Lesser and Kadri Tastan, "EU–Turkey Relations: Steering in Stormy Seas" (no 31, GMF 2018) <www.gmfus.org/sites/default/files/publications/pdf/EU-Turkey%20Relations-%20Steering%20in%20Stormy%20Seas_July%2031.pdf> accessed 14 October 2019.
[63]Copenhagen European Council, 21–22 June 1993, Presidency Conclusions <www.europarl.europa.eu/enlargement/ec/cop_en.htm> accessed 14 October 2019.

The issue with the above criteria is who defines democracy, rule of law, human rights and protection of minorities and who determines the appropriate criteria to assess these factors? Within the European Union, all of these factors are "subject to political assessment"[64] by the European Commission and European Council. This leaves Turkey in a precarious position as they are always subject to the political will and perception of others rather than any consistent procedure. In fact, it is surprising that in several European countries, the term "minority" is defined widely. Russia and Luxembourg do not recognise the term "national minority" and Belgium believes it is a matter of foreign policy whilst Estonia defines the term with reference to ethnicity, language, culture and religion and North Macedonia lists several groups such as Albanians, Turks and Serbs who are classed as minorities.[65] One may ask if there is no consistency in defining who is a minority, how does one go on to judge whether a group's human rights are being infringed? And if the term "minority" is not recognised by major member states but they are still part of the European Union, then isn't this a violation of the Copenhagen criteria?

Therefore, it is more plausible to argue that membership of the EU is based more upon indeterminate political criteria than a stringent adherence to the rule of law, human rights and protection of minorities. If this is the case, then it is important for textbooks to highlight the alternative discourse that is present within the history of Europe to present an objective viewpoint about the way in which the European Union functions.

The need to reform law schools

Western law schools operate on a very narrow and inaccurate paradigm of their own history; they fail to consider the historical and continuing influence of Islamic law on contemporary legal concepts. This is not to say that Western law is not dynamic in itself but rather to suggest a holistic understanding of its origins would enable us to tackle some of the most important challenges law schools face today. For example, the relationship between Islamic and Western law, the rise of Islamic finance as a major practice area, the understanding and implementation of human rights and access to justice with regard to asylum seekers and refugees. Instead of a dichotomised approach to these issues, a shared understanding would help us come up with creative solutions that draw upon the resources of both Islamic and Western law. It would also nurture critical-minded lecturers that are capable of challenging norms and adapting to new problems. I therefore propose that law schools need to consider the following scholastic reforms:

- Decolonising law syllabuses by introducing textbooks and articles from Islamic legal heritage.
- Creating new modules that deeply explore the history and relationship between Islamic law and Western law.

---

[64] "Briefing No 23: Legal Questions of Enlargement" <www.europarl.europa.eu/enlargement/briefings/23a2_en.htm> accessed 14 October 2019.

[65] See Panayote Elias Dimitras, "Recognition of Minorities in Europe: Protecting Rights and Dignity" (Minority Rights Group International 2004) <https://minorityrights.org/wp-content/uploads/old-site-downloads/download-47-Recognition-of-Minorities-in-Europe-Protecting-Rights-and-Dignity.pdf> accessed 14 October 2019.

- To invite and draw upon Muslim scholars and institutions who are proposing new frameworks to solve contemporary legal problems.[66]

The goal of these three reforms is to nurture legal scholars and students to question the historical and philosophical presumptions that are embedded in the law books they study. This would cause a much-needed shift in valuing other knowledge systems that have an equal contribution to make in a world marred by conflict and war and at times, fuelled by misconceptions of each other's religion, race, culture and heritage. It also helps subvert any strategy of power that seeks to intellectually and psychologically dominate others through knowledge control and the production of conceptual binaries that could in fact work together.

Disclosure statement

No potential conflict of interest was reported by the author.

[66]Apart from well-known scholars such as Abdullahi an-Na'im, Wael Hallaq, Khalid Abu El-Fadl, Abdulaziz Sachedina, Mashood Baderin, Mohsen Kadivar, Anver Emon and many others, institutions such as the Al-Mahdi Institute (www.almahdi.edu) are very active in initiating dialogue between Muslim and Western legal scholars. They have published a book with Brill that may be of interest to readers in this field; my humble chapter deals with comparing jurisprudential techniques in both Islamic and English law: "From Theory to Practice: English Case Law as an Additional and Evidentiary Holistic Tool for the Derivation and Operation of Law in Shi'i Usul al-Fiqh" in Ali-Reza Bhojani, Michael Bohlander and Laurens de Rooij, *Visions of Shari'a: Contemporary Discussions in Shi'i Legal Theory* (Brill 2019) 83–128.

Index

Abdul-Ahad, Ghaith 61
academics 2–3, 6, 13, 59, 65, 67–68, 70–72, 91, 98
Adebisi, Foluke 40
Adisa, Gamba 79
Africa 18, 69, 81, 86–87
Agozino, Biko 24
Ahmed, Sara 12
Ahmet, Akile 10
Algerian War 106–7
Allison, Graham 59
Ambedkar, B.R. 18
anachronism 52, 54
Anghie, Antony 83
anti-racist movement 76
anti-racist space 15, 17, 19
Anzaldúa, Gloria 18
Aquinas, Thomas 99
Aristotle 99
Ashcroft, Bill 55
attainment gap 76, 91
Austin, John 83
Australia 4, 28, 36–37, 39, 41, 46, 83
Averrorism 98–99

Bacon, Roger 99
Black British Feminism 80, 86–88, 90, 92
Black British students 72
Black Feminism 80, 84–86, 88
Black feminist decolonisation 88–89; of curricula 90–93
BlackLivesMatter movement 74
Black people 68–73, 77, 81, 86
Black students 67, 72, 91–92
Black women 84–87, 90
Blaut, James 55
Boisard, Marcel A. 107
British state 23–24, 27, 29, 42

campus rebellions 12, 15, 20
Canada 1, 4
capital accumulation 3
Carbado, Devon 70
Chakrabarty, Dipesh 55–56
Christianity 99–100, 104
class 7, 25, 27–29, 31–33, 42–46, 85–87
Collingwood, R.G. 51
colonial discipline 2–3
colonial governance 23
colonial history 21, 31, 34, 50, 59, 62, 72, 106
colonialism 1–2, 5, 24, 27–30, 34, 49–50, 55, 58, 76, 87
coloniality 2, 9, 81, 84
colonial legacies 24, 49, 57, 62
colonial penality 25
colonial power 36, 41, 43
colonial university 9, 15
colonisation 2, 5, 28–29, 37, 39, 44, 48, 51, 56, 65–69, 75–77, 105, 107
colour 8, 11–14, 16–20, 43, 54, 64, 66–69, 71–78
colour-blind attitudes 70–71
colour-blind meritocracy 64–65, 70–71
colour-blindness 59, 65–66, 77
command theory 83
commercial treaties 106
common law jurisprudence 39
conference 3, 5–6
corporate actors 28
courage 7, 9, 15–20
crime 21–30, 33–34
criminal justice agencies 23
criminal law 21–22, 25, 28, 82
criminology 6, 21–25, 27, 33–34
critical pedagogy 37, 47
critical race theory (CRT) 9, 43, 45, 66, 68, 74, 84–85

critical whiteness studies 19
Crown Prosecution Service (CPS) 27
curriculum 2, 19, 22, 24–25, 34–35, 46, 64–68, 70, 72, 75–76, 84, 89, 91; decolonise 65

Davies, Margaret 58–59
decolonial space 7–10, 13–18, 20
decolonial whiteness 12
Doharty, Nadena 12
Dorsett, Shaunnagh 39

empowerment 18, 76
epistemological fragility 53
epistemologies 2, 35, 37–40, 66, 82, 86, 88
ethnicity 57–59, 108
Eurocentrism 54–56, 105
European Union 82, 105–8
exploitation 10, 14, 56, 58, 61–62, 86

Ferguson, Niall 59
Fisk, Catherine 50–51
France 102, 106–7
Freire, Paulo 67

Garofalo, Raffaele 25–26
Gaudiosi, Monica M. 102–3
gender 40, 65–66, 77, 85, 87
Gibb, Sir Hamilton 98–99
Gibson, Ross 38
Gillborn, David 12
Ginzburg, Carlo 52–54
global designs 2–3
global white supremacy 4
Gordon, Lewis 82
Gordon, Robert 50–51
Griffin, Gareth 55
Gulati, Muti 70
Gunaratnam, Yasmin 58

Hall, Stuart 27, 58
Harris, Angela 85
Hirsch, Afua 65, 68
Hoggart, Richard 30
human rights 24, 26, 34–35, 42–43, 48, 62, 106–8

Ibbetson, David 52
Ibn Rushd 99
Ibn Sina 99
Icaza, Rosalba 88
identities 54, 56, 58, 64–65, 67–69, 72, 74, 77, 92
imperialism 2, 26, 47, 55–56, 86–87
India 22, 24–25, 27, 31–32, 57, 61
Indigenous communities 39
Indigenous law 39–40, 43
Indigenous people 1, 24, 28, 37, 40–41, 43
institutional racism 11–12
international law 24, 36–38, 46, 48–49, 83, 107
International Slavery Museum 25, 29
international terrorism 24
intersectionality 84–85, 88
Islam 95–96, 98–104, 107
Islamic law 6, 94–96, 98, 101, 103–4, 106–8
Islamic legal scholasticism 101–4
Islamoromia 101

Joseph-Salisbury, Remi 12
jurisprudence 3–4, 6, 35, 39, 42, 45, 48, 82–83, 95–96
justice 21, 24–29, 35, 42–43, 48–49, 69, 108

knowledge 2, 4, 8–10, 12–15, 30–31, 40–41, 45–46, 50, 53, 66–68, 70, 84, 88–90, 92

Labourdonnais, Mahé de 58
legal epistemologies 35–36, 38–41, 45–46, 48
legal genocide 24
legal theory 42, 95–98
Lombroso 23
London 8, 43–44
Lowenthal, David 52

McIntosh, Peggy 66
McMillan, Mark 39, 41, 46
McVeigh, Shaun 39, 44
Madriaga, Manuel 12
Makdisi, George 101–2
Mangin, Charles 81
Manning, Kathleen 71
Mantena, Karuna 83
Massey, Doreen 38
Matias, Cheryl 11
Mauritius 6, 50, 57–62
Mbembe, Achille 82
meritocracy 64–66, 70–72
migrants 60–61
Mill, John Stuart 83
mistrust 9–10, 12, 99
Modern Slavery Act 62
Modiri, Joel 3–5, 75

Morant Bay 25, 28–29
Morris, Katie Boudreau 41, 47
Muslims 8, 94–95, 98–99, 103

neoliberal colonial university 9–10
neoliberal university model 10
neoplantations 11
North-Coombes, Daniel 59

Onyeozili, Emmanuel 24

paternalism 76
penal law 22–23, 26
Pilger, John 28
Pillai, K.S. 23
plantation politics 11–12
Plato 99
political blackness 87
power 13–16, 19–20, 28, 33–34, 37–39, 42–43, 45, 67–68, 70, 74, 77–78
property crime 33
punishment 21, 23, 25–26, 29

Qur'an 96–99, 101

race 19, 22–23, 25–28, 30, 32–35, 45–48, 58–59, 65–66, 71, 74, 77, 81, 85–87
racial diversity 71
racialised students 92–93
racism 5, 8–9, 17, 22–23, 26–29, 31, 34, 58–59, 62, 66, 73, 87, 91
racist patriarchy 79
rationality 65–66
repressive technology 24
#RhodesMustFall movement 70

scholasticism 100–1
Scotland 35–36, 41, 47
self-decolonisation 65, 68, 72, 75
settler–Indigenous relationship 36
silencing/silence 1, 7, 9, 14–15, 18–20
Smith, Barbara 84
Smith, Linda Tuhiwai 4, 40
social realities 56, 93
Spivak, Gayatri Chakravorty 54, 56
Squire, Dian 12
staff of colour 8, 11–13, 16
staff relationality 12, 20
Stage, Frances 71
structural racism 14, 16, 26, 34
students of colour 14, 64, 67–68, 71, 73, 77

Tan, Seow Hon 38
Tate, Shirley Anne 15, 18
Teaching Evaluation Framework (TEF) 10, 76
Teelock, Vijaya 51, 59
Tiffin, Helen 55
toolkits 73, 76
transgressions 5, 26
transitionality 89, 92
transnational solidarities 18, 87
trust 7, 9, 12–18, 20, 30, 82, 103
Tuck, Eve 42, 46–47
Tuitt, Frank 12

Unger, Roberto 85

Vázquez, Ronaldo 88
violence 4, 16–18, 25, 27, 38–39, 45, 49, 75

Walia, Harsha 41
waqf (charitable endowment) 102–4
war crimes 42–43
Western historiography 54–56
Western law 94–95, 100, 105, 108; schools 101, 108
White, Hayden 53
white academics 15, 64, 67
White Jesus 73–74
whiteness 3, 9–10, 12–20, 34, 67, 72
white women 79, 84–86
Williams, Bianca C. 12
Williams, Robert A. 4, 43
workers 60–61
working identity 70

Yang, K. Wayne 42, 46–47
Young, Michael 65

Zachariah, Benjamin 57

Kolibri 360 GmbH
Ferdinand-Jühlke-Straße 7
99095 Erfurt, Deutschland
produktsicherheit@kolibri360.de